The
CHURCH
&
ABORTION

In Search of New Ground for Response

Essays by:

RUTH S. BROWN
MICHAEL J. GORMAN
STANLEY HAUERWAS
WILLIAM H. WILLIMON

PAUL T. STALLSWORTH, *general editor*

Abingdon Press/Nashville

THE CHURCH AND ABORTION

This book is printed on recycled, acid-free paper.

Library of Congress Cataloging-in-Publication Data

The Church & abortion : in search of new ground for response : essays / by Ruth Brown, Michael J. Gorman, Stanley Hauerwas, William H. Willimon ; Paul T. Stallsworth, general editor.
    p.   cm.
Includes bibliographical references.
    ISBN 0-687-07852-0 (acid-free paper)
    1. Abortion—Religious aspects—United Methodist Church (U.S.)—Congresses.   2. Abortion—United States—Congresses.   I. Stallsworth, Paul T.
II. Brown, Ruth (Ruth S.)   III. Title: Church and abortion.
HQ767.35.C48   1993
241'.6976'08827—dc20   92-40691
                                              CIP

93 94 95 96 97 98 99 00 01 — 10 9 8 7 6 5 4 3 2 1

MANUFACTURED IN THE UNITED STATES OF AMERICA

CONTENTS

To My Parents

PREFACE

Irst to origins. This book emerges from a conference on the Church and abortion that was held at Edenton Street United Methodist Church, Raleigh, North Carolina. The four conference papers and the four panel presentations, which are contained herein, connect, in one way or another, with The Durham Declaration, which is also contained. The Durham Declaration, which was written by United Methodists for United Methodists (and others), is an attempt to address the problem of abortion in a specifically Christian, and in an identifiably churchly, way. The origins of the Declaration itself are reported at the beginning of chapter 6.

It is important to note at the outset that United Methodism is the communal context of this book and its origins. For over twenty years The United Methodist Church has been squarely confronted with the problem of abortion. And for over twenty years The United Methodist Church, a self-avowedly "inclusive" church, has attempted, in its official position on abortion, to appeal to the maximum number of Methodists. Methodism's attempted compromise on abortion is "on the books," so to speak, in the intentionally ambiguous paragraph on abortion in the church's Social Principles, which is located in The Book of Discipline. That paragraph, in apparent contradiction, both acknowledges "the sanctity of unborn human life" and supports "the legal option of abortion" (Paragraph 71G, The Book of Discipline, 1988).

One of the unfortunate results of the church's attempt at compromise is that some quarters of United Methodism have decided that abortion is no longer a topic open for discussion. In these quarters, it is deemed too divisive to discuss. Another

5

observable result is that when United Methodist discussions of abortion do push to the surface, they are often dominated and driven by the political language and arguments that are current in American culture.

All in all, it should be said that, though the church's leadership has tried to reach a compromise position on abortion, United Methodism has yet to achieve a settled position on abortion. United Methodism's abortion compromise seems under endless discussion. And, interestingly, the official United Methodist position, as articulated in the *Discipline*, has been moving in a protection-of-the-unborn direction over the past decade.

As expected, the 1992 General Conference of The United Methodist Church addressed the problem of abortion, yet again. Three points about the 1992 General Conference actions on abortion should be made. First, the overwhelming majority of petitions and resolutions that were submitted to General Conference—by boards, agencies, annual conferences, local congregations, groups, ministers, and members of the church—were decidedly "pro-life" in orientation. Most of these petitions and resolutions were disapproved by the conference's legislative committees. Still, this legislative churning is an indication that the unsettled state of the church on abortion will not soon vanish. Second, in evenhanded fashion, the 1992 conference amended Paragraph 71G of the 1988 *Discipline* to include the following: "We call for the church to provide nurturing ministries to those persons who terminate a pregnancy. We encourage the church to provide nurturing ministries to those who give birth." It has been suggested by some that this amendment is related to the lines of argument generated by The Durham Declaration. And third, by a surprisingly narrow margin (485-448), the conference turned back a move to remove all United Methodist support (including participation by the General Board of Church and Society and the Women's Division of the General Board of Global Ministries) from the Religious Coalition for Abortion Rights (RCAR). RCAR, on the grounds of "religious liberty," lobbies federal and state governments to legislatively maintain, or move towards, practically absolute abortion rights. (To the amazement of some, during plenary debate, RCAR was described by a couple of conference delegates as "moderate" on abortion.) In spite of the General Conference vote on the church's relationship to RCAR, the matter is not a "done deal," for it has been referred to Judicial Council for further investigation and deliberation. In all likelihood, even the Judicial Council's decision, whatever its content, will not put this issue to rest in the United Methodist household.

It should be understood that the current United Methodist position on abortion is out of step with historic and ecumenical Christianity. Through the ages the Church has consistently resisted abortion and offered ministry to those tempted by abortion. Also, the vast majority of the churches in the world today—from evangelical Protestant to Roman Catholic to Orthodox—are, more or less, in line with classical Christian teaching on abortion. For some reason (namely, the power of philosophical liberalism, which has been turned into an ideology of choice and applied to all spheres of life), oldline American Protestantism, including United Methodism, has insisted on a more "open" attitude toward abortion. Therefore, on the matter of abortion, this church has broken, and continues to break, ranks with the catholic, or universal, Church. Hence, The Durham Declaration.

Those who have helped to make this book possible hope against hope that *The Church and Abortion* will assist in informing, and perhaps reforming, the heart and mind of The United Methodist Church regarding abortion. With that strong hope, this text is offered to United Methodists (and others) for study—particularly in church school classes, in evening studies, in Bible studies, in youth groups, in discipleship groups, and in ministers' gatherings. It is to be humbly admitted that *The Church and Abortion* does not pretend to include all the answers regarding the difficult subject matter at hand; however, its approach just might open up, for The United Methodist Church (and other churches), a new and more fruitful way to respond to the problem of abortion.

This book begins with The Durham Declaration. From there, William H. Willimon invites the reader to approach abortion from a baptismal-congregational standpoint. Then, Michael J. Gorman, in an essay that is sure to become a point of reference in the abortion debate within the churches, reflects on the consensus of early Christian texts that pertain to abortion. The following chapter, which tackles the usual arguments on abortion from an aggressively Christian position, is by Stanley Hauerwas. Next, Ruth S. Brown addresses ministerial possibilities in response to the abortion problem. An account of the conference conversation, which was lively from beginning to end, concludes the book.

ACKNOWLEDGMENTS

This project has depended upon too many persons to list. However, for starters, there is Richard John Neuhaus, whose public ministry and friendship are gifts beyond measure. Also, there are Steven Paul Wissler and Paul R. Crikelair who have been steady colleagues; continuing conversation with them decisively shaped the direction of the Declaration. Thanks to J. Malloy Owen III, who was instrumental in broadening the initial conversations that hammered out the Declaration; and to Gregory K. Jenks and Alan P. Swartz, who wrote two of the earliest drafts of the Declaration. Also, thanks is due Michael J. Gorman, who was the first to suggest that a conference on the Declaration would be in order. Through generous grants, Christ United Methodist Church of Memphis, First United Methodist Church of Houston, Frazer Memorial United Methodist Church of Montgomery, and Pine Castle United Methodist Church of Orlando helped to make the conference possible.

Heartfelt thanks goes out to M. Randall Baker, my district superintendent, who is a faithful colleague in the ministry of the Church. Also, to the churches I seek to serve on the Creswell Charge—the Creswell, Holly Grove, and Mount Hermon congregations—for striving to hear, to trust, and to live out the gospel of Christ.

Finally, I owe a debt of gratitude too large to contemplate to my beloved wife, Marsha, and to the children—Ryan, Paige, and Matthew—who have been entrusted to us. They have provided the seldom acknowledged good cheer (through conversations over the evening dishes, and through basketball and softball games played out in the front yard), understanding, and love that are required by a project such as this.

Not intending to sound like a country-and-western singer who, after having just won an award from the Country Music

Association, is saying a few words to a concert hall full of people, I end on a hopeful note: May this book, and the conversation that it sparks, glorify the God who, always and everywhere,
is most faithful—even when God's world is faithless, and even
when the people of God are unfaithful.

Reverend Paul T. Stallsworth
Pentecost 1992
Creswell United Methodist Charge
Creswell, North Carolina

Chapter 1

THE DURHAM DECLARATION:

TO UNITED METHODISTS ON OUR CHURCH AND ABORTION

INTRODUCTION

United Methodists, abortion is testing our church. Abortion is testing our church today as deeply as slavery tested our church in the nineteenth century. Abortion is stirring up great confusion and exposing deep conflicts in our community of faith. This condition continues, in part, because The United Methodist Church has not addressed the problem of abortion theologically. Our church has been content to debate abortion with the merely political terms that American society has made available. This is an insufficient response to a historic test.

The time has come to call The United Methodist Church to a scriptural, theological, and pastoral approach to abortion. This we will attempt to do. As United Methodists addressing United Methodists on abortion, we hereby declare our beliefs, confess our sins, and pledge ourselves to a new life together.

DECLARING OUR BELIEFS: OUR BODIES, CHRIST'S BODY, AND CHILDREN

Contemporary culture insists that we own our bodies and that we have a right to do with them whatever we want. However, we United Methodist Christians declare that this is false.

We believe that we are not our own (I Cor. 6:19). We do not own our selves or our bodies. God owns us. "It is he that made us, and we are his" (Ps. 100:3, RSV used throughout The Durham Declaration). Furthermore, it is God who "bought [us] with a price," (I Cor. 6:20) with the life of Jesus sacrificed on the Cross.

And it is God who sanctifies us to be "temple[s] of the Holy Spirit" (I Cor. 6:19).

We believe that, through faith in Christ and baptism into His Body, God has made us "members of Christ" (I Cor 6:15). That is, we are incorporated into the Body of Christ, the Church. "So we, though many, are one body in Christ, and individually members one of another" (Rom. 12:5). Partaking of the Bread and the Cup, we as members of the Body of Christ demonstrate that we are not accountable merely to ourselves. We are accountable to God and to one another. That means we care and provide for one another as brothers and sisters.

We believe that caring and providing for one another includes welcoming children into the family of the Church. As members of the Body of Christ, we know that children—those who are hidden in the womb and those who are held by the hand, those who are labeled "unwanted" and those who are called "wanted"—are gifts from God. In this we follow the example of our Lord, who, during his earthly ministry and in the face of opposition, welcomed children to his side (Matt. 19:13-15). And we conform to the example of the early Church, which—though living in the midst of a pagan empire that casually practiced abortion and abandoned children (usually to slavery, prostitution, or death)—helped to provide refuge for unwanted little ones and their needy parents.[1]

We believe that God welcomes us through the outstretched arms of his Son on the Cross: "The arms of love that compass me / Would all mankind embrace" (Charles Wesley, "Jesus! the Name High Over All"). Because this God has welcomed us into the Church, we can likewise welcome the little ones.

CONFESSING OUR SINS: OUR REBELLION, COMPROMISE, AND FEAR

We confess that we have rebelled against God. We have rejected the light of Christ and turned to the darkness of the world. We have denied—by thought, word, and deed—that we belong to God.

We confess that we have often compromised the gospel by submitting to the seductions of society. We have exchanged the message of salvation in Jesus Christ for a false message about human potential. We have capitulated to extreme self-involvement and self-interest. Neglecting the call to discipleship, we have treated matters related to marriage, sex, and children as if they were merely life-style questions. We have lived as if the Church is simply another voluntary association of autonomous individuals. We have lived as if the Church is not the Body of Christ in which we "bear one another's burdens" (Gal. 6:2). We have lived as if we are our own, not God's.

We confess that, as a part of the People of God, we have not honestly confronted the problem of abortion. Fearing division, we have removed abortion from the concerns of our church's mission. Thereby our church has reduced the abortion problem to private choice and to just another issue for partisan politics. Therefore, in our churches we have selectively applied the truths of God's ownership of us and God's gift of children. We have neglected our sister who is in a difficult pregnancy and offered her no alternatives to abortion. Rarely have we offered, through our ministries, the forgiving love of Christ to the woman who has aborted. We have not hospitably welcomed the so-called "unwanted child" into our churches and families. We have not challenged or worked to alter the mindset and social realities that sustain our abortion-conducive culture.

PLEDGING OURSELVES TO A NEW LIFE TOGETHER: OUR PROMISES

1. We pledge, with God's help, to become a church that unapologetically proclaims the message of salvation in Jesus Christ to a world that is usually apathetic and sometimes antagonistic.

2. We pledge, with God's help, to practice and to teach a sexual ethic that adorns the gospel. Christian discipleship includes, though is not limited to, the ordering of God's gift of sexuality. Sexual discipline requires, at minimum, "fidelity in marriage and celibacy in singleness."[2] According to biblical teaching, sexual relations outside the boundaries of "fidelity in marriage and celibacy in singleness" are manifestations of sin that call for repentance and reconciliation. This ordering is a part of the excellent way of Christian discipleship. It stands over against

the jungle of modern sexuality, which is most evident in our society's inability to hold men sexually accountable.

Biblically based sexual discipline should be directly and consistently advocated—by our church's bishops, district superintendents, clergy, parents, church schools, publishing programs, colleges and universities, hospitals, and children's homes and agencies—among United Methodist children, youth, and adults. In addition, the church should teach the responsibilities for men and women that accompany sex. The church should strongly condemn sexual promiscuity.

3. We pledge, with God's help, to teach our churches that the unborn child is created in the image of God and is one for whom the Son of God died. This child is God's child. This child is part of God's world. So the life of this child is not ours to take. Therefore, it is sin to take this child's life for reasons whether of birth control, gender selection, convenience, or avoidance of embarrassment.

4. We pledge, as people of a community whose sins are forgiven by God, to offer the hope of God's mercy and forgiveness to the woman who has obtained an elective abortion. God's forgiveness and healing are also to be offered to those who have assisted a woman in aborting and now repent.

5. We pledge, with God's help, to become a church that hospitably provides safe refuge for the so-called "unwanted child" and mother. We will joyfully welcome and generously support—with prayer, friendship, and material resources—both child and mother. This support includes strong encouragement for the biological father to be a father, in deed, to his child.

6. We pledge, with God's help, to honor the woman who has, under difficult circumstances, carried her child to term.

7. We pledge, with God's help, to call our church's boards and agencies to end their support of pro-choice political advocacy and also to develop ministries that support women in difficult pregnancies.[3]

8. We pledge, with God's help, to encourage United Methodist-related hospitals to adopt medical ethics guidelines that are protective of the unborn child and mother.

9. We pledge, with God's help, to consider how our church should best apply discipline to her members who reap profits,

small and large, from the advocacy and performance of elective abortion.

CONCLUSION

In a society that is so obsessed with material success and pleasure that it wantonly destroys over 1.5 million of its unborn children every year, we United Methodists hear the words of our Lord, "Let the little children come to me, and do not hinder them" (Matt. 19:14). We heed these words of Jesus by ordering our life together so that we can joyfully receive the children.

To accomplish this task, to meet the massive test that abortion now poses to The United Methodist Church, we rely only upon Christ until his Kingdom comes. It is Christ who promises, "My grace is sufficient for you, for my power is made perfect in weakness" (II Cor. 12:9). He, above all else, is to be trusted.

NOTES

1. Drawing from James Tunstead Burtchaell's "Opening Statement in Debate" [*Commonweal* 114 (November 20, 1987), p. 663], L. Gregory Jones notes, "The new Christian faith [of the early Church] set four prophetic imperatives before those who would live in the Spirit and fire of Christ, four disconcerting duties that would distance them from Jews and Romans alike. . . . The fourth imperative was that in addition to those children orphaned by their parents' deaths, they were to protect the infant—unborn or newborn. This imperative is expressed in *The Didache, The Instruction of the Twelve Apostles* (the oldest Christian document we possess outside the New Testament): '. . . you shall not murder a child by abortion, or kill a newborn . . .' " [from "Christian Communities and Biomedical Technologies" in *Bioethics and the Beginning of Life*, Roman J. Miller and Beryl H. Brubaker, eds. (Scottdale, Pa.: Herald Press, 1990), p. 116]. Furthermore, the primitive Church's firm opposition to abortion is expressed in some two dozen early Christian documents.

Second- and third-century sources on the Christian refusal to abandon children and the Christian imperative to rescue the abandoned include: *Epistle to Diognetus* 5, Aristides' *Apology* 15, *Who Is the Rich Man That Is Saved?* by Clement of Alexandria, *Apology* 39 by Tertullian, *Epistle of Polycarp to the Philippians* 6:1, and *Ignatius to the Smyrneans* 6:2.

Also, see Michael J. Gorman's "Historical Perspectives" in Miller and Brubaker. Gorman writes: "Beginning in the late fourth century under the leadership of both bishops and monks, orphanages and foundling homes (for abandoned and exposed children) were established throughout the Christian world. From its birth the Christian Church had been characterized by its compassion for children. Even the earliest Christians frequently rescued abandoned children and raised them in a Christian family. The foundling homes became visible symbols of Christian compassion for unwanted children in the communities of Europe and the East" (p. 136).

2. This wording appears in the chapter on ordained ministry in *The Book of Discipline* (Nashville: The United Methodist Publishing House, 1988), Par. 404.4e and several other locations. The Christian's fidelity in marriage or celibacy in singleness is best understood as a manifestation of divine grace that is given for the good of the church, the family, and the man/woman.

3. Charles W. Hubbard's challenge—that The United Methodist Church secure $50 million to build and support regional crisis pregnancy centers across the U.S.—should be taken seriously by our church. See *Christian Social Action* (April 1990), pp. 28-30. Our boards and agencies should be much more serious about supporting and/or providing adoption services as well.

—————— Chapter 2 ——————

THE MINISTRY OF HOSPITALITY

William H. Willimon

William H. Willimon is the Dean of the Duke University Chapel and Professor of Christian Ministry at Duke Divinity School.

I n one of my congregations, we had a not-so-unusual occurrence. A sixteen-year-old woman had war with her single-parent mother. The mother worked as a waitress in a restaurant. Her daughter began "running around with the wrong crowd." There was some evidence that the daughter herself was "the wrong crowd." The mother came to me in desperation. What could she do with her daughter? I talked with the daughter, who was sullen and uncommunicative. Yet, from conversations with mother and daughter, I became convinced that something had to be done.

Shortly thereafter I was visiting a retired public-school librarian one afternoon. She lived by herself in a small but adequate house. She was about seventy. During our conversation, she mentioned something about being lonely and feeling old and out of touch. Quite without thinking, I told her some of the particulars of the mother-daughter situation and asked her if she would be willing for this teenager to come live with her for a time. Quite without thinking, she said, "Yes."

That woman kept that teenager for nearly two years. Both of them were challenged, tested, strengthened, and enriched in the process. After two years, the teenager had grown and the mother had gotten her life better adjusted, so the teenager had returned home.

During those two years, every Sunday, the three of them sat together on the same pew at church. Only later did I, as a pastor, realize that what I had just witnessed was an act of baptismal fidelity.

A BAPTISMAL PROBLEM

In an earlier article on The Durham Declaration[1], I noted that the opening section of the Declaration deals with baptism, "a subject which has been curiously omitted from much abortion debate." I would like to take a portion—a rather uninspiring, humble portion—of the United Methodist Baptismal Covenant, as a source for some pastoral, evangelical thoughts about abortion. The church has always taught *lex orandi, lex credendi*—that is, the law of prayer precedes the law of belief. If you want to know what the church believes about a subject, listen to how the church prays. Our liturgy, the service we render to God in our worship, and our ethics, the service we render to God in daily life, are one in the liturgical, ethical attempt to bend our lives, and to have our lives bent, toward God. So if we are asked to account for what we believe about humanity, it is only natural that we should refer to baptism, that peculiar Christian means for human renovation through which "we are initiated in Christ's holy church . . . incorporated into God's mighty acts of salvation and given new birth through water and the Spirit."[2]

Where to begin thinking about that act now named "abortion" in that rite called baptism? In the opening act of repentance and renunciation of sin? The Durham Declaration is being baptismal when it opens with a call to confession of our sin with regard to abortion and its victims. Is the charge to the candidates "to resist evil, injustice, and oppression in whatever forms they present themselves"?[3] What sort of evil, injustice, or oppression is abortion? Baptism teaches us to name what injustice and evil look like, not by the world's definitions, but through the peculiar lens of the gospel. It is not immediately apparent why Christians might be concerned about something like abortion, until we have first dealt with the peculiarity of the gospel. Baptism's demonstration of that peculiarity begins to be suggested when the service speaks of our being engrafted into a church that "Christ has opened to people of all ages, nations, and races."[4]

I shall bypass possibly fruitful sources of baptismal thought about abortion such as the prayer of thanksgiving's recollection of "Jesus, nurtured in the water of a womb"[5] and move instead to a less dramatic part of the United Methodist baptismal service, the "Commendation and Welcome." What if we began thinking about abortion on the basis of what each of us says before God and the congregation when someone is baptized? This is our promise:

> We give thanks for all that God has already given you
>   and we welcome you in Christian love.
> As members together with you
>   in the body of Christ
>   and in this congregation
>   of The United Methodist Church,
> we renew our covenant
>   faithfully to participate
>   in the ministries of the church
>   by our prayers, our presence,
>   our gifts, and our service,
> that in everything God may be glorified
>   through Jesus Christ.[6]

I have come to see that this closing of the baptismal service, in which the congregation welcomes the newly baptized person by naming what God has done in that person's life and by pledging their own responsibility and hospitality, is one of the most important parts of the service. In welcoming the newly baptized person, the congregants quite rightly demonstrate that this act of hospitality is a fitting occasion to renew their covenant to the ministry of the church. The church's core ministry, in the light of this Commendation and Welcome, is the ministry of hospitality.

The church is that place where, through baptism, we are made to stand and to welcome people whom we do not even know. Thereby, in that act of hospitality, our own covenant with Christ is renewed as we are reminded of the astounding hospitality that Christ has shown toward us. From this perspective, the Christian life is simply long, often painful, forever surprising training in the art of hospitality, welcoming the stranger as we strangers have been welcomed by God in Christ. Much more could be said about what baptism does to us and for us but, for present purposes, particularly as we consider abortion, note that baptism transforms us into those who, in the name of Christ, offer hospitality to strangers.

CANDIDATES FOR WELCOME

When we think of strangers, particularly within the context of the society we have created called the United States of America, it would be difficult to think of more difficult strangers than children. I have a hunch that the U.S. has declining birth rates because we have enough sense to see that children are the ultimate threat to some of the most dearly cherished and widely held values of our society. Children are inherently needy, dependent, demanding, and difficult. No one can threaten me as deeply as my own children. They are the ones who will ultimately bury me. There they sit, impatiently waiting to take the future from me and live it as they will, rather than as I want. When I am dead, they will be the only ones left to tell about my life and name who I have been. About the worst you can say about my children is that they look a great deal like me and my values, only more so. What reasonable adult would willingly look into the searching, naked stare of such a mirror? Abortion is a no-confidence vote in ourselves and our ability to welcome children.

Yet for all their threat, children also offer the possibility that I just may be a more interesting human being than I think. In the context of baptism, children offer the evangelical possibility that we just might be a more faithful church than we think. The faithful willingness to be open to the gift of children is an evangelical vote of confidence in God and ourselves, a courageous witness that we have been given the gifts needed to receive even those as potentially disruptive as children.

Openness to children is roughly similar to Jesus' command for us to love our enemies and to pray for those who persecute us (Matt. 5:44). We resist loving our enemies because we doubt that we have been given the gifts to do so yet. Only if we are bold enough to attempt loving our enemies might we discover that the Holy Spirit really does have the power to produce the sort of disciples Jesus deserves. Among the many difficult things demanded of us in baptism, among the Spirit's many gifts offered to us, is the demand for hospitality.

If children are difficult to receive, let us also admit that women and men who have personally experienced abortion are also difficult to receive. Too many of those who have had abortions feel lonely, guilty, and alienated, in great part because they have been told by an unfaithful church that abortion is "a private issue," "a personal choice." Therefore, if they are in pain and heartache after abortion, it becomes a terribly lonely pain. Having told them that their abortion was a private, personal matter, we render their pain private and personal as well, something to be borne alone. This is sub-Christian. In the church, we invite people's pain to go public, to be brought to church and shared with others. This is where true healing begins.

Can the church truly welcome the woman who has had an abortion? Can we expose ourselves to her pain as a searchingly honest mirror of our own failures? If we can, we will soon learn that abortion is not freedom for women. We will learn that abortion is freedom for men, and that it is a freedom won for men at the cost of a terrible loneliness for many of the women who experience abortion.

When Kathy Rudy tells me that the primary reason women whom she has interviewed give for having an abortion is, "I had no other option," it makes me want to ask some hard questions about my church. Where were we when the woman was agonizing over her options? Rather than provide options, options provided by our own sacrifice and commitment, we made abortion a private, personal issue. We described abortion in such a way so that, no matter how the discussion ended, it would end in such a way that we would have no responsibility for this woman or her decision. It is not pleasant to be reminded by this woman of the failures of our church. Therefore, it will take an act of baptismal courage to make our churches truly hospitable to women who have had abortions.

STORIES OF BAPTISMAL HOSPITALITY

I received a telephone call at 7:00 A.M. Had I heard? Thomas was in jail. DUI. The police had him and a two-hundred-dollar bail was required. I got the call just before I was to leave for the men's Bible Study and Prayer Breakfast. After our Bible study, I told the other men about Thomas being in jail. They knew him. They knew his mother. His father had died when the boy was

21

very young. His mother had been trying to raise him as well as she could but, at seventeen, he had become quite unmanageable.

Some of the men offered to go with me to the jail. We got there. They emptied their wallets and bailed him out. Out in the parking lot of the jail, we had prayer with him. They told him that they loved him. John Jones took Thomas home with him for a few days. A week later, George took Thomas with him to his AA meeting.

This is a story of baptismal hospitality with implications for abortion.

Some years ago, the church I was serving began an emphasis on evangelism. We were a downtown church that had been in rapid membership decline over the last two decades. We desperately needed new members. Several evangelism outreach programs were begun. In one program we trained two teams of retired persons to be what we called "Baby Visitors." We drew a map of our neighborhood. They took as their goal the visitation of every baby born within a one-mile radius of our church. We received six new couples and one single-parent mother from our efforts in one year. As it turned out, there were people out there having babies by themselves. God, of course, did not intend for people to have babies alone. People are grateful for anybody, even a church, who is excited about their new baby. They are anxious to receive support and guidance.

This is a story of baptismal hospitality with implications for abortion.

I spoke in a Baptist church. I had some unkind things to say about fundamentalists. During the discussion after my talk, a young woman told me, "I don't know much about fundamentalists and moderates. All I know was that I was an Episcopalian all my life. My grandfather was an Episcopal priest. My husband and I were active in a nice Episcopal church in Memphis. Then I committed the unforgivable sin."

"Unforgivable sin?" I asked.

"Yes," she continued. "Didn't know it at the time. But I committed the unforgivable sin by giving birth to a baby with Down syndrome. Our priest visited me in the hospital and immediately urged us not to take the baby home with us. Nobody from the church called. When we showed up four weeks later with our new baby at the church, people treated us like we had some kind of disease. Nice people, in such a nice neighborhood, didn't do things like this. I cried all night after our first Sunday back at that church. Then I went to a big Baptist church down the road. I think they are what you would call 'fundamentalist.' All I know is that, when we walked in that church, they treated us like royalty, told us that they had just sent a woman over to Nashville to be trained to work with special children. I plan to stay a Baptist the rest of my life."

This is a story of baptismal hospitality with implications for abortion.

Of course, such stories also have implications for how we deal with the homeless, the sick, the infirm, and everyone else whom we are taught to avoid as strangers. We are Christians, which means we are always out there trying to treat everyone like family, trying to baptize them into Christ and his Church. In baptism, we say that we do not believe in "one-parent families." We do not believe in "two-parent families." We believe that, in today's world, it is so tough to make a Christian out of a baby that it takes almost the whole congregation to do it. We do not believe that biology makes parenthood. Baptism makes parenthood and, in the Church, by baptism, we are often shocked by who our real parents are. We name them on All Saints' Day. In baptism, we receive the stranger, not simply because thereby we think that we might help the stranger, but more importantly because, "Inasmuch as ye have done it unto one of the least of these . . ." (Matt. 25:40 KJV), we believe we are thereby meeting the Christ, the One who came to us as a baby, a stranger in a manger, who was also our Savior. We have Bible stories that tell of people who received strangers and, to their surprise, were entertaining angels, unawares. These are stories of baptismal hospitality with implications for abortion.

In this paper I have not presented a "theology of abortion." Nor did I get into debates over abstractions like "right to life" or "freedom of choice." I do not have a theology of abortion; what is more, I do not really want one. You see, I am a Methodist, a Wesleyan. We do not really have a "theology." What we have is better. What we have is a set of practices, a bunch of habits, laid upon us in baptism; they teach us to construe the world in certain peculiar ways. We Wesleyans do not begin with intellectual debates, definitions, head trips. We begin with habits. We believe that the only divinity worth having is Father John's "practical divinity"—that is, embodied, practiced, visible, ordinary enactment of the gospel.

So, on Sundays we often turn, in the front of our hymnals, to a service we call baptism. A stranger stands up in front of us. We tell the stranger that Christ died for him or her, and then we make a few trial runs trying to call this stranger "brother" or "sister." The service, reminding us that we were once greater strangers to God than this person, makes the congregation stand up and promise to receive this stranger into the family. If we do the service often enough, go over the words enough, practice the moves, by the grace of God, we might get good at it. We might end up better people than we would have been if we had been left to our own devices. We might be more of a church than even we wanted or God promised. Thereby, in the light of baptism, this national crisis of abortion would have become, in God's amazing grace, a gracious invitation for us to own up to our baptism, to become the Church.

NOTES

1. "A Uniquely Christian Stand on Abortion," *The Christian Century*, February 27, 1991, pp. 220-21.

2. *The United Methodist Hymnal* (Nashville: The United Methodist Publishing House, 1989), p. 33.

3. Ibid., p. 34.

4. Ibid.

5. Ibid., p. 36.

6. Ibid., p. 38.

———— Chapter 3 ————

AHEAD TO OUR PAST:
ABORTION AND CHRISTIAN TEXTS

Michael J. Gorman

Michael J. Gorman teaches early Christianity and moral theology at The Ecumenical Institute of Theology at St. Mary's Seminary and University in Baltimore, and he serves as Assistant Director of the Council for Religion in Independent Schools in Washington, D.C.

According to a sympathetic but critical reviewer, The Durham Declaration "makes a significant contribution to the church's reflection on the abortion issue . . . by attempting to address it from a distinctly biblical and theological perspective while avoiding the language of rights that dominates all political discourse in the United States and the abortion debate in particular."[1] This "distinctly biblical and theological perspective" is an effort to view the abortion issue in a broad, rather than a narrow, framework that is shaped by the ethics of the New Testament.[2] The Declaration is also a deliberate attempt to reappropriate historical Christian texts and practices within this New Testament framework.[3]

The aim of this essay is first to identify and explore the significance of the Declaration's New Testament foundations, then to examine specific early Christian attitudes and practices regarding abortion and closely related issues, and finally to suggest some ways in which the texts and practices discussed speak to the church today. Before pursuing those tasks, however, we must first acknowledge the New Testament's silence on abortion per se and determine the proper questions to ask in pursuing a perspective on abortion grounded in the New Testament.

A. ASKING THE RIGHT QUESTIONS

The silence of the Bible generally, and the New Testament specifically, on abortion has been a source of distress for many Christians. It has led to a wide range of interpretations—from assertions of early Christian ignorance of or apathy toward the issue, to belief in divine apathy ("If the Bible is silent, can God care?"), to attempts at discovering prooftexts that demonstrate Christianity's (and God's) condemnation or approval.

As we will see below, there are historical reasons for the New Testament's silence on abortion. Ironically, when this silence is understood historically, it proves to speak quite loudly. For now, however, our task is to engage the New Testament in the discussion of a topic that it does not directly address.

To use the Bible in facing the abortion issue is no simple task. We must first recognize, however, that even if the canon spoke a clear No! on the abortion issue, the church would almost certainly still have a debate on its hands. In the face of the canon's silence and the likelihood of debate even if it spoke clearly, we must phrase our questions properly. Two appropriate questions are the following:

1. To what kind of ethical perspectives and moral life does the New Testament bear witness through its narratives and arguments, its claims and convictions, and how should that affect our view of abortion?

2. To what kind of moral lives and views of abortion have earlier generations of Christians been called through their reflection on scriptural, especially New Testament, texts and themes?

The first question reflects a particular view of the role of the New Testament in Christian moral thinking: it shapes our basic perspectives and molds our individual and corporate character (virtues actualized in deeds). The second reflects a belief in the Church universal and in the Holy Spirit as the One who has inspired the Church in other times and places. The focus of this paper will be on the early Church, which has a claim to unique importance because of its proximity to Jesus and the apostles and its pervasive influence on later Christian faith and practice.

The thesis of this paper, and the contention of The Durham Declaration, is that the New Testament, both in principle and as embodied in early Christian communities, leads us away from abortion, toward protecting and welcoming the unborn, and toward providing compassionate care to those in need.

B. THE FRAMEWORK OF THE DECLARATION: FUNDAMENTAL AFFIRMATIONS

The Durham Declaration rests on three fundamental New Testament convictions:

1. We are not our own, but God's.
2. We are members of Christ and of one another.
3. Welcoming children is an integral part of Christian discipleship.

In other words, the Declaration is built on basic New Testament teachings about the human body, the Christian body, and children. To these three, a fourth should be added that is necessary to complete a New Testament framework for viewing any moral concern:

4. The age of shalom (peace) has begun in the life of Jesus and his Church.

In its own way, each of these convictions was and is a radical challenge to normal perceptions of reality and morality.

1. THE HUMAN BODY

The Declaration begins with an appeal to Paul's fundamental text on the nature of Christian freedom with respect to the body (I Cor. 6:12-20). In Paul's day, many Corinthian believers associated Christian faith with the realm of the spirit alone, not the body. They believed that no bodily action—not even sex with prostitutes, probably at pagan temples—could adversely affect their relationship to God and, therefore, that they had the right and freedom to do whatever they wished with their bodies.[4]

Paul counters these attitudes by asserting the importance of the physical body as an integral part of the self: the body—or the embodied self—will be raised on the last day, is a "member" of Christ's body, is a temple of the Holy Spirit, and—most impor-

27

tantly—has been purchased (a metaphor for the ransom of slaves) by God through the death of Christ. "You are not your own [lord]; you were bought with a price," says the apostle. For Paul, Christians do not belong to themselves; they have relinquished control of their lives and bodies to God who redeemed them, to Christ who died for them, and to the Spirit who indwells them. They no longer live for themselves, looking to assert their own rights, but for the God to whom they now belong.[5] Freedom consists not of asserting one's desires and rights—this is giving opportunity to the "flesh" (see Gal. 5)—but of yielding one's body, soul, and mind in service to God and others.

St. Paul's perspective, that Christians belong not to themselves but to Another, is at the core of his Christian ethics and is echoed in various ways throughout the entire New Testament. Such a vision is fundamentally at odds with the world, where individuals seek to exercise ultimate control over their own lives and bodies, using their bodies not for divine service but for self-service. Like the Corinthians, many contemporary Christians, both male and female, believe that they are their own masters, with the right to do as they please with their own bodies.

The New Testament perspective is completely antithetical to this notion. It is, therefore, completely antithetical to the claim that there is a divinely granted right to engage in whatever form of sexual activity one prefers, or to choose an abortion because there is a divinely given gift of freedom to do with one's body whatever one wishes to do. For Paul and the New Testament generally, that is not freedom but slavery. The Pauline/New Testament perspective, therefore, challenges two of the dominant cultural values of our day that have too often been absorbed and advocated by spokespersons for the church—virtually unlimited sexual and procreative freedom.[6] The Declaration begins with a direct assault on these two pillars of the case for abortion.

2. THE CHRISTIAN BODY

The assertion of absolute choice in sexual and procreative matters is a manifestation of our culture's obsession with individual rights that impacts the Christian church in other ways, too. The Declaration continues with a statement of the nature and mission of the church in contrast to this rampant individualism. For many Christians, the church is still a voluntary association of individuals who convene weekly but who actually exist as individuals responsible for and to themselves alone. When serious emotional, financial, or other kinds of problems develop, many Christians look at best to the pastor or other church leaders, at worst to no one in the church at all. A woman's unplanned or crisis pregnancy is perhaps the most isolating and difficult of such experiences.

The New Testament, in such passages as I Corinthians 12 and Ephesians 4, depicts the church as a human body that consists of interdependent parts—connected people who are mutually supportive, responsible, and accountable; people who learn and practice the ways of Christ together in community. Moreover, the kind of love that exists in this fellowship extends to others in need. It was this kind of vision of community that motivated early Christians to band together to serve one another and the world. In fact, the text of I Corinthians 12 inspired Basil of Caesarea, a monk of the late fourth century, to organize monasteries whose purpose was not merely to pray and study but to serve.[7] This led to the establishment of the first Christian hospitals, hospices, and orphanages.

3. CHILDREN

Few episodes in the life of Jesus had as much impact on the shape of early Christian morality and ministry as did the well-known encounters between Jesus and the children. When Jesus' disciples attempt to prevent children from approaching their master (Mark 10:13-16 and parallels), Jesus' reaction is startling: he is indignant.[8] It is only in historical perspective that Jesus' attitude and action, and its effect on the early Christians, can be fully understood.[9] Among the Jews, rabbis classified children along with the deaf, mute, and mentally deficient. Elsewhere in the Roman Empire children were thought of as no better. In Roman custom and law children were understood to be the property of their father. Furthermore, fathers had the legal right to discard or kill children who were of the "wrong" (i.e., female) gender or who were "imperfect"—deformed or handicapped.[10] If exposed at the local garbage heap, the children who survived would often be picked up to be made into slaves or prostitutes.

In this context it is very clear that the Kingdom of God reverses normal human values. People taken to be of no value by other people take on infinite value.[11] Jesus' treatment of children inaugurated nothing less than the elevation of their status from the marginalized, even the disposable, to full persons. Moreover, Jesus made it clear that one's reception of children is determinative of one's reception of Jesus, his Father, and the Kingdom: "whoever welcomes one such child in my name welcomes me, and whoever welcomes me, welcomes not me but him who sent me" (Mark 9:37).

Jesus did not, however, limit his full humanization of the marginalized to children; he similarly elevated the status and value of women. Although the early Church did not always implement Jesus' example fully, it was extremely sensitive to the needs of women and children who most often were not otherwise treated as neighbors: widows and orphans. As the Declaration notes (footnote 1 in chapter 1), the early Church's commitment to the orphan and widow was universally recognized and exercised.

4. SHALOM

The Durham Declaration is built primarily on the three New Testament themes discussed above. One additional biblical and early Christian theme that is absolutely essential to any description of Christian morality is that of shalom, which means "divine peace and justice" or "eschatological wholeness." The Hebrew Scriptures point forward to a time when violence will cease and when peace, security, and justice will reign. Jesus taught that this promised age of shalom, often referred to as the Kingdom (or Reign) of God, broke into history in his ministry and was to take effect in the common life of his followers: "Blessed are the makers of shalom" (Matthew 5:9). The New Testament and other early Christian writers share this conviction, too, believing that the age to come, the age of peace and justice, has begun in the life and mission of Jesus and in the community of his followers who are assured and empowered by the Resurrection and Spirit of Jesus.[12]

Beginning in the first century, Christians lived in peace by refraining from violence, fighting spiritual rather than military battles (see Ephesians 6), and engaging in concrete acts of peacemaking. This continued into the second century and beyond, when writers such as Justin Martyr (c. 150) expressed their conviction that the Christian community fulfilled the prophecies of a time of shalom in the following manner: "We who were full of war and murder of one another and all evil have everywhere changed our instruments of war—swords into plows and spears into farm tools."[13] This moral vision was articulated in a world that was, in the estimation of the early Church, engulfed in violence and bloodshed. Early Christians perceived in their culture an "interlocking directorate of death"[14], which stretched from abortions to gladiator spectacles to crucifixions. Their response was to forsake violence and to form a new army engaging in a new form of warfare: "an army without weapons, without warfare, without bloodshed . . . [supporting] old men, orphans dear to God, widows . . . ;"[15] "[our] warfare is justice itself."[16] One form of this "warfare" called shalom was opposition to abortion, and support of children left to die.[17]

C. ABORTION AND THE EARLY CHRISTIAN MORAL VISION

The four basic New Testament perspectives we have examined—on the human body, the Christian body, children, and shalom (justice/non-violence)—helped create a moral vision that produced a distinctly Christian attitude toward abortion and related issues (e.g., exposure and infanticide), as well as a ministry to women and children in need that complemented their attitude.[18] The Christians' new perspectives confirmed and strengthened the opposition to abortion that already existed among their Jewish forebears, whose condemnation of induced abortion (with the exception of therapeutic abortion) is heard in Philo, Josephus, and popular early Jewish moralists.[19]

Building on its Jewish heritage, the early Church was, indeed, a vocal opponent of abortion. The unified voice of early Christian writings on the abortion issue includes some of the most important documents of the early Christian era. In fact, the three earliest documents that mention (and condemn) abortion were extraordinarily popular and widely distributed, considered by many of those who read and heard them to be inspired Scripture: the Didache, The Instruction of the Twelve Apostles; the Epistle of

Barnabas; and the *Apocalypse of Peter*. These Jewish-Christian documents from the late first and early second centuries were included in many of the early Christian canons (lists of inspired Scripture) and were, therefore, functionally part of the New Testament for many Christians for many years.[20] Eventually these writings were found to be post-apostolic and were therefore omitted from the final New Testament canon, henceforth categorized as "profitable," but not authoritative, texts.[21]

It is clear, therefore, that Christian leaders, who used the criterion of orthodoxy as one essential test of a document's claim to a place in the canon or in the Church's devotional life, considered opposition to abortion to be an orthodox Christian belief. It is important to recognize, then, that early Christianity saw rejection of abortion as consonant with the teachings of Jesus and the Christian gospel.[22]

The early Christian attitude toward abortion can be analyzed in several ways. One helpful way to approach the topic is to look at the Church's perspectives on four of its dimensions: the unborn child, the act of abortion, the moral agent who obtains or performs the abortion, and pastoral responses to abortion.

1. THE UNBORN CHILD

It is clear from early Christian texts, first of all, that the early Christians lived under the conviction that newborn and unborn children were special creations of God and were, in fact, their neighbors. The two earliest (late first-century and very early second-century) Christian texts on abortion, found in the *Didache* and the *Epistle of Barnabas*, discuss it in their exposition of the command to "love your neighbor as yourself" (or, as *Barnabas* has it, "more than yourself"). They say, "Thou shalt not murder a child by abortion, nor kill the newborn."[23] In the latter part of the second century, Athenagoras proclaimed that the fetus is the "object of God's care," while Clement of Alexandria argued that the unborn and newborn are the "designs of providence."[24] Tertullian, trained in rhetoric and probably law, challenged the Roman legal view of the fetus as an appendage of the mother,[25] arguing that the fetus is already a person "while as yet the human being derives blood from other parts of the [mother's] body for its sustenance."[26] In other words (despite

Roman and even Jewish law[27]), dependence on the woman does not render the fetus merely a part of the woman.

This high view of the newborn and unborn was part of the general Christian "neighborization" of people who were deemed nonpersons by much of the surrounding culture. Personhood and human value were determined in the Greco-Roman world by those in power: adult males who were heads of households. Christianity claimed that those under the power of a householder (wife; children, both born and unborn; and slaves) were "neighbors"—in philosophical language, "persons"—and, if members of the household of faith, even brothers and sisters.[28] Thus the unborn constituted one group among several whose status as "neighbor" was recognized and proclaimed in the Church.

It is clear, furthermore, that in the early Church the unborn's status as neighbor, or person, was independent of its biological development.[29] Greek concern about the time at which an embryo or fetus receives a soul (and thus becomes a "person" in some sense), and even Jewish concern about the legal status of the fetus, are completely absent from the earliest Christian discussions.[30] When the issue of fetal development is finally raised in the late fourth century, it is dismissed by Basil (the Great) of Caesarea as irrelevant to the abortion question: "She who has deliberately destroyed a fetus has to pay the penalty of murder. And there is no exact inquiry among us as to whether the fetus was formed or unformed."[31]

2. THE ACT OF ABORTION

Early Christianity, believing the embryo or fetus to be the special creation of God, a neighbor claiming the Christian community's love, could draw no other conclusion about abortion than this: that it is a violation of the commandment "Thou shall not kill."

In the above-cited earliest Christian texts, the *Didache* and *Epistle of Barnabas*, abortion is termed murder and prohibited categorically in the form of a commandment: "Thou shalt not. . . ." Other writers of the early Church echo this perspective:

> We say that women who induce abortions are murderers, and will
> have to give account of it to God. (Athenagoras, a great apologist

33

of the late second century, Plea 35 in Early Christian Fathers, ed. Cyril C. Richardson et al. [New York: Macmillan, 1970])

In our case, murder being once for all forbidden, we may not destroy even the fetus in the womb. To hinder a birth is merely a speedier homicide. (Tertullian, late second-/early third-century theologian and apologist, Apology 9.6 in The Ante-Nicene Fathers, vol. III, ed. Alexander Roberts and James Donaldson [New York: Charles Scribner's Sons, 1903])

There are women who . . . [are] committing infanticide before they give birth to the infant. (Minucius Felix, early third-century theologian, Octavius 30.2 in The Octavius of Minucius Felix, ed. G.W. Clarke, Ancient Christian Writers, vol. 339 [New York: Newman Press, 1974])

[Abortion is] murder before the birth . . . or rather . . . something even worse than murder. (John Chrysostom, Homily 24 on Romans in Nicene and Post-Nicene Fathers, vol. XI, ed. Philip Schaff [New York: Charles Scribner's Sons, 1899])

The early Church did not, however, see the act of abortion as a unique act, an act in isolation. Rather, it viewed abortion as a manifestation of the social injustice, drive to power over the powerless, and violence of its culture.[32] It was these things that Christ and thus the Christian community rejected; abortion was perceived as part of the "interlocking directorate of death" that was the antithesis of Christian existence. Furthermore, following the example and teachings of Jesus, Christians redefined power and greatness as love and service. They saw abortion and infanticide as acts of raw power by the powerful over the powerless.[33] In all early Christian texts about children—unborn, newborn, and others in the household—and in Christian dealings with children, there is a radical rejection of the Roman notion that the father owned his children and thus held the right to determine their fate—life or death.

3. THE MORAL AGENT

What did early Christians say about those who obtain or perform abortions? Objectively, they held, the agent is guilty before God. Although some of the early texts specifically reproach only the woman who obtains an abortion, from the earliest times Christianity also condemned those who perform abortions. The prohibition "Thou shalt not murder a child by abortion" applied equally to those who obtain and perform abortions. Basil summarizes the Christian position: "Those, too, who give drugs causing abortion are murderers themselves, as well as those receiving the poison which kills the fetus."[34] For Origen and Hippolytus in the third century, obtaining (and, implicitly, performing) an abortion called into question the reality of one's Christian faith.[35] Shortly thereafter, when the penitential system developed, women who aborted were barred from communion and church life, at first until their death and then, as penalties were relaxed, for a period of ten years.

Subjectively, it was felt by some early Christians that the act of abortion had psychological and spiritual effects on the moral agents involved. According to Clement, "women who |abort|. . . abort at the same time their human feelings."[36]

4. PASTORAL RESPONSES

The early Christian pastoral responses to abortion have been hinted at in earlier sections of this paper. Broadly speaking, this response had three dimensions: (1) prophetic preaching and teaching; (2) administration of grace and penance; and (3) provision of assistance to the poor, including orphans. This last aspect, though not directly addressing abortion, is perhaps the most significant.

The earliest Christians did not open counseling centers to dissuade women from seeking abortion or men from exposing deformed children. The Christians did, however, feel compelled to "rescue the orphan"—the child abandoned on the dung heap—and to provide for the poor, especially poor women.[37] Although these ministries did not focus on "problem-pregnancy situations" in the modern sense, there can be little doubt that the Church's practices would remind the Church's poor and others in crisis situations that they were not alone in the world; that children mattered to the Christian community and therefore to God; and that their needs would be met, their children cared for. In all probability, this would provide encouragement and hope to those who might consider abortion. This kind of social ministry was, according to all historians of early Christianity, one of the chief reasons for its success in the ancient world. The Church's ministry to the poor and orphans, then, was a sign of life and of grace—a "sacrament." While the precise impact of this kind of ministry is impossible to measure, it is clear that the Church's protection and improvement of human life was both an essential part of its self-understanding and an influential presence in the pagan world.

D. ONCE AGAIN: THE NEW TESTAMENT'S "SILENCE"

At the outset of this paper it was noted that the New Testament does not speak *about* the abortion issue. Nonetheless, in the early Church, the life and teachings of Jesus, the gospel message, and the Scriptures did speak *to* the abortion issue. Ironically, the former reality is largely the result of the latter. That is, the canonical New Testament is accidentally silent; there is abundant testimony to what the early Christians heard about abortion in the gospel message. Christian opposition to abortion was so universal and so integral to the Christian vision—as it had been to the Jewish—that its absence from the canon when it was "closed" in the late fourth century would be neither remarkable nor immediately noticeable. Indeed, long before the canon was finalized, Christian opposition to abortion had been institutionalized by being included in the Church's canon law.[38]

When we consider the New Testament, we must remember that it was not carefully planned and assembled by a committee attempting to prepare a comprehensive guide to the Christian way. It is an occasional collection of occasional documents. As in the case of certain other acts—most notably infant exposure and infanticide, which are not explicitly condemned in the New Testament either—early Christianity's natural rejection of endangering or taking human life sometimes found explicit expression in its literature, and sometimes did not. The New Testament's lack of a text on abortion may be surprising, but its meaning must not be misinterpreted. Understood in its historical context, it is evidence of early Christianity's clear and consistent rejection of abortion.

E. CONCLUSION AND DIRECTIONS

What the early Christians heard in their assemblies was a message of non-violence and compassion that spoke directly to the issue of abortion. The result was a church with a moral vision and character that may well be needed in the contemporary church. This can be summarized in the following list of the virtues found among the early Christians: holiness in sexual matters, horror of bloodshed, "neighborization" or "humanization" of non-persons, and compassionate help to the needy.

Are these virtues not the essence of biblical ethics, the New Testament vision, and the Christian moral tradition? If they are, and if the Christian message is not to be ignored or distorted, then the contemporary church's mandate seems clear: to move away from abortion, toward protecting and welcoming the unborn, and toward providing compassionate care to those in need.

The greatest challenge to commonly held beliefs, both within and beyond the church, will be to convince both men and women that they have no absolute right over their own bodies, and absolutely no right over the lives and bodies of others. Many men still believe they have power over women and children, the power to use and abuse, even the power of life and death. It is often they—as fathers, boyfriends, husbands, employers—who urge unwilling women to choose them over a child *in utero*. At the same time, many women have learned to believe that they have absolute power over their bodies and thus also over the child within. In law, philosophy, theology, and custom, the ancient paternal power of life and death over the unborn has been transferred to women. Nothing short of radical conversion from these reincarnations of Roman power over women and the unborn will alter the current situation. This conversion, like divine judgment, must begin with the household of God.[39]

The greatest challenge to the moral life of the Church and its various institutions will be to find the imagination and will to become channels of life and grace, where the "orphan and widow" are welcome.[40] This life will be dedicated not only to rescuing the unborn from death but also to improving the quality of life for women and children. For, to paraphrase I John, how can we say that we love the unborn whom we have not seen, if we do not love the already born whom we have seen?[41]

NOTES

1. Barry Penn Hollar, "Increasing the Burden on Women: An Appreciative, but Critical Response to the Durham Declaration on the Abortion Issue," *Christian Social Action* (July/August 1991): 28.

2. It is, in Professor Hauerwas's words, a statement of "those deep |specifically Christian| convictions that make our rejection of abortion intelligible" (Stanley Hauerwas, "Abortion: Why the Arguments Fail," in ed. James T. Burtchaell, *Abortion Parley* |New York: Andrews and McMeel, 1980|, p. 325).

3. Harvard historian George H. Williams once suggested that a long-standing general Protestant silence on fetal value and abortion is due to the general Protestant zeal for the principle of *sola Scriptura*, which has often led to ignorance of all early Christian beliefs and practices not specifically recorded in the canonical New Testament ("Religious Residues and Presuppositions in the American Debate on Abortion," *Theological Studies* 31 |1970|: 42). The United Methodist Church's Social Principles do refer to the Christian tradition about abortion, but only to the (implicitly common and most significant) instances of establishing criteria for choosing abortion under certain circumstances. The text of the Social Principles (Paragraph 71G) reads, in part: "In continuity with past Christian teaching, we recognize tragic conflicts of life with life that may justify abortion, and in such cases support the legal option of abortion under proper medical procedures."

4. Furthermore, some Christians may have been attracted to this particular form of sex because of the frequent connection in pagan religion between sexual experience and experience of the divine. Certain recent understandings of sexuality that equate, or nearly equate, erotic love with divine love are more pagan than Christian.

5. Implicit in I Corinthians 6 and explicit elsewhere (e.g., Romans 6), is the Pauline conviction that prior to Christian faith people are slaves to sin and to self; afterwards they are "slaves"—willing servants—to righteousness and to God.

6. It is difficult to miss the similarity between some of the current theologies of sexual and procreative freedom and the errors described in II Peter 2:17-22, where certain leaders "uttering loud boasts of folly . . . entice with licentious passions of the flesh those who have barely escaped from those who live in error, promising them freedom while

they themselves are slaves of corruption; for by whatever you are overcome, to that you are enslaved" (vv. 18-19 RSV [with alterations]).

7. See his *Longer Rules* 7.

8. The Greek word used in Mark's narrative (10:14) to describe Jesus'
extreme anger at his disciples is used of Jesus nowhere else in the New
Testament.

9. For a readable account of the situation, see Hans-Ruedi Weber,
Jesus and the Children: Biblical Resources for Study and Preaching (Geneva:
World Council of Churches, 1979). See also Ian Stockton, "Children,
Church, and Kingdom," *Scottish Journal of Theology* 36 (1983): 87-97.

10. A famous letter testifying to the common acceptance of such attitudes has been preserved from the first century b.c. In that letter a husband who is away on a military assignment writes to his wife, who is
about to give birth to their child, as follows: "If it is a male child, let it
live; if it is female, cast it out." (The text of this letter may be found in
various sources, including C.K. Barrett, *The New Testament Background:
Selected Documents* New York: Harper & Row, 1961, p. 38.)

11. The infinite worth of children is finally revealed in the cross. As
the Declaration, drawing on Karl Barth, affirms, even the unborn child
"is one for whom the Son of God died" (see Karl Barth, *Church Dogmatics*
III/4 [Edinburgh: T. & T. Clark, 1961], p. 416).

12. Professor Hauerwas summarizes this view and its relationship to
the protection of human life as follows: "As members of such a kingdom [of peace], moreover, we are pledged to extend God's peace
through the care and protection of his creation. . . . Therefore the Christian commitment to the protection of life is an eschatological commitment. Our concern to protect and enhance life is a sign of our confidence that in fact we live in a new age in which it is possible to see the
other as God's creation. . . . The risk of so valuing life can only be taken
on the basis of the resurrection of Jesus as God's decisive eschatological act. . . . Peace has been made possible by the resurrection." (*The
Peaceable Kingdom: A Primer in Christian Ethics* [Notre Dame, Ind.: University of Notre Dame Press, 1983], pp. 88-89).

13. *Dialogue with Trypho* 110 (author's translation).

14. The term is from Daniel Berrigan, who decries this country's
"interlocking directorate of death that binds our culture, stretching
from the Pentagon to the abortion clinic" (interview, "The Dying and the
Unborn," *Reflections* reprint, n.d.).

15. Clement of Alexandria, *Who Is the Rich Man That Is Saved?* (author's translation).

16. Lactantius *Divine Institutions* 6. 20. 10. 15-17 (*The Ante-Nicene Fathers*, vol. VII, ed. Alexander Roberts and James Donaldson [New York: Charles Scribner's Sons, 1899]).

17. For further discussion of the meaning of shalom and its relation to abortion, see Michael J. Gorman, "Shalom and the Unborn," *Transformation* 3 (January-March 1986): 26-33.

18. For a more detailed description of this entire topic, see Michael J. Gorman, *Abortion and the Early Church: Christian, Jewish, and Pagan Attitudes in the Greco-Roman World* (InterVarsity and Paulist, 1982) and G. Bonner, "Abortion and Early Christian Thought," in ed., J.H. Channer, *Abortion and the Sanctity of Human Life* (Greenwood, S.C.: Attic Press, 1985), pp 93-122.

19. No known ancient Jew supported abortion except to save the mother's life. For further discussion, see Gorman, *Abortion and the Early Church*, chapter 3.

20. The failure to recognize the widespread authority, canonicity, and use of early Christian documents condemning abortion is one of the chief reasons for erroneous conclusions like that of Beverly W. Harrison in *Our Right to Choose: Toward a New Ethic of Abortion* (Boston: Beacon, 1983), who argues for a "widespread silence about abortion in early Christian writings" (p. 134). She further contends that "apart from [the *Didache*], . . . explicit denunciations of abortion, separate from views on the irreducible responsibility to procreation, are rare in early Christianity. [Historian John] Noonan's claim . . . that 'by 450 [C.E.] the teaching on abortion East and West had been set out for four centuries with clarity and consistency' is doubtful at best, though the fragmentary evidence on the question makes dogmatism either way impossible" (p. 133). Ironically, by failing to recognize the role of the developing canon, Harrison is guilty of limiting herself to the "methods of intellectual history" rather than "the newer methodologies of social and cultural history" (p. 120)—the same error Harrison attributes to "traditional" historians of the Christian position on abortion.

21. These three works are completely unknown to most people today because they are not part of the New Testament canon we have inherited from Athanasius (A.D. 367). All three of these writings, however, were still frequently considered part of the New Testament even into the fourth century, and all were read for inspiration even after they were officially excluded from the canon in 367. When many people think of the New Testament, they think of a first-century collection of inspired Christian books. It is true that most, if not all, of the books that make up the New Testament were written in the second half of the first cen-

tury. But these were not the only Christian writings considered by early Christian congregations to be inspired. Nor was the New Testament assembled and published all at once some time in the late first or early second century. Rather, its formation was gradual, beginning perhaps in the late first or early second century and ending (in most churches) in the late fourth. In other words, the 27-book New Testament as a whole, as a collection, is not really a first-century publication but a fourth-century publication of first-century writings.

22. It should also be noted that the eventual omission of the *Didache*, *Barnabas*, and *the Apocalypse of Peter* from the canon was not due in any way to their view of abortion, which was accepted throughout the Church.

23. *Didache* 2:2 and *Epistle of Barnabas* 19:5 (author's translation).

24. Athenagoras, *A Plea Regarding Christians* 35 (*Early Christian Fathers*, ed. Cyril C. Richardson *et al.* [New York: Macmillan, 1970]); Clement of Alexandria *Tutor* 2.10.96.1 (author's translation).

25. Justinian *Digest* 25.4.1.1 and elsewhere.

26. *Apology* 9.6 (*The Ante-Nicene Fathers*, vol. III).

27. Although Jews opposed abortion and viewed the fetus as God's creation, they did not believe that one became a person legally until birth.

28. This is implied, for example, in the household tables of Ephesians 5–6 and Colossians 3–4.

29. People in antiquity believed that the unborn becomes truly human at a variety of stages in its development—conception, 40 or 90 days of gestation, birth, and perhaps even after birth. The criteria for determining humanity were also somewhat varied, with possession of a soul being the chief criterion. In other words, philosophical import was attributed to biological development; moral status was a function of psychological and biological status. But even the attainment of a certain stage of development was deemed insufficient for unborn, or even newborn, life to have value. Its value was determined primarily on a utilitarian basis, either individualistic or social. That is, the value of the fetus was assigned by a controlling power, either the father or the state, according to his or its own desires and needs.

30. The absence of such distinctions is especially remarkable because the early Christians' Old Testament (the Greek Septuagint [LXX]), under the influence of Greek philosophy, had mistranslated the Hebrew of Exod. 21:22-23 and erroneously introduced the notion of formed and unformed fetuses into the text, implying by the different penalties assigned that only the abortion of a formed fetus is murder.

(The Hebrew words "no harm . . . harm" were translated as "no form . . . form.") Thus the LXX could easily have been used to distinguish human from non-human fetuses and homicidal from non-homicidal abortions, yet the early Christians, until the time of Augustine in the fifth century, did not do so.

31. *Letter* 188.2, written c. 374 (Saint Basil, *Letters*, vol. II, trans. Agnes Clare Way, Fathers of the Church, vol. 28 [New York: Fathers of the Church, 1955]). Basil, it should be noted, also stressed leniency and grace for the crime. In the twentieth century, Dietrich Bonhoeffer would echo the same sentiments in his *Ethics* (New York: Macmillan, 1955, pp. 175-76): "To raise the question whether we are here concerned already with a human being or not is merely to confuse the issue. The simple fact is that God certainly intended to create a human being and that this nascent human being has been deliberately deprived of his life. And that is nothing but murder." Bonhoeffer also emphasizes that "the guilt may often lie rather with the community than with the individual" (p. 176).

32. Abortion is rejected along with other forms of social injustice in the *Didache* and the *Epistle of Barnabas*. In Tertullian's *Apology* and Athenagoras' *Plea* it is rejected as a form of lethal violence, to which Christians are consistently opposed in theory and practice.

33. Cf. John Calvin, in his commentary on Exodus 21:22-23: "If it seems more horrible to kill a man in his own house than in a field, it ought surely to be deemed more atrocious to destroy a fetus in the womb before it comes to light" (*Commentary on Exodus*).

34. *Letter* 188.8.

35. Origen refers to such people as "so-called Christians."

36. *Tutor* 2.10.96.1 (author's translation). This sentiment has been echoed by others in our own day, including Mother Teresa, who has said that those who cause abortions kill not only the child in the women but their own compassion. If it seems that some of the early texts put an undue amount of guilt and burden on women, we should perhaps respond not by condemning the early Christians but by recognizing the breadth of guilt and of negative effects in our own culture and churches. As both pro-life and pro-choice advocates have said, we do indeed live in an "abortifacient" (Paul Ramsey) or "abortion-conducive" (Virginia Ramey Molenkott) culture, and the practice and acceptance of abortion in such overwhelming numbers for so long have undoubtedly de-sensitized us to human pain and human life and allowed us to continue accepting violence as a solution to problems.

37. The phrase "the orphan and the widow" was probably a generic term for all women and children left without a protector and provider,

whether by death or abandonment. Of the many early Christian admonitions to and descriptions of care for the orphan and the widow, The Durham Declaration (footnote 1) notes seven. These, as well as other texts, claim that Christians "do not abandon their offspring" (*Epistle to Diognetus* 5) but do "save the orphan" (Aristides, *Apology* 15). They also exhort Christians to "uphold the rights of the orphan" (1 *Clement* 8:4), never "neglecting the widow or orphan or one that is poor" (Polycarp, *Epistle to the Philippians* 6:1). (All quotations are author's translations.)

38. At the Councils of Elvira (c. 309) and Ancyra (314).

39. Although space does not permit detailed discussion, it seems to me that recent feminist analysis of the Bible confirms rather than contradicts the thesis of this paragraph. Two of the main concerns of feminist analysis are (1) feminine images of God in the Bible; and (2) criticism of traditional biblical interpretations that find justification for power and domination. An understanding of God and Christ as our life-giving, protecting mother would logically lead to divine imitation in the form of compassion for, rather than destruction of, children. Similarly, criticism of male-generated justifications for power ought to lead to an ethic of all-inclusive compassion that would be critical of all, not just male, forms of power over the powerless. For pro-life feminism, see, among others: Denise Lardner Carmody, *The Double Cross: Ordination, Abortion and Catholic Feminism* (New York: Crossroad, 1986); Sidney Callahan, "Abortion and the Sexual Agenda," *Commonweal* (April 25, 1986): 232-38 and reprinted in Robert M. Baird and Stuart E. Rosenbaum, eds., *The Ethics of Abortion: Pro-Life vs. Pro-Choice* (Buffalo: Prometheus Books, 1989), pp. 131-42; and Gail Grenier Sweet, ed. *Pro-Life Feminism: Different Voices* (Toronto: Life Cycle Books, 1985).

40. In addition to the obvious forms of ministry—counseling centers, food and clothing assistance, shelters, orphanages, adoption, childcare—the Church will have to be creative to meet the overwhelming challenge. As an example, shortly before his death, Professor (and United Methodist layperson) Paul Ramsey suggested to me in a private conversation that churches initiate a new form of "godparenting" in which young, economically disadvantaged, or otherwise needy mothers/parents who could not adequately provide for children would temporarily (or even permanently) place them in the care of people within their church. Human life would be spared, contact between parent(s) and child would continue, and the church would function as the church. Ramsey discusses this idea briefly in (oddly enough) his *Speak Up for Just War or Pacifism* (University Park, Pa.: Pennsylvania State University Press, 1988), p. 146.

41. I wish to thank Rev. John Heinsohn, former colleague in ministry and pastor of Kingston (N.J.) Presbyterian Church, for suggesting the paraphrase of I John in a sermon.

Chapter 4

ABORTION, THEOLOGICALLY UNDERSTOOD

Stanley Hauerwas

*Stanley Hauerwas is Professor of Theological Ethics at
Duke Divinity School.*

I am going to start with a sermon. Every once in a while you get a wonderful gift. Recently a former student, who is now a Presbyterian minister, mailed to me a copy of a sermon on abortion. I could not do better than offer this sermon and an ethical commentary on it. The author of the following sermon is the Reverend Terry Hamilton-Poore, formerly the chaplain of Queens College, Charlotte, North Carolina, and now of Kansas City, Missouri.

TEXT AND SERMON

The text for the sermon is Matthew 25:31-46, from the Revised Standard Version.

"When the Son of man comes in his glory, and all the angels with him, then he will sit on his glorious throne. Before him will be gathered all the nations, and he will separate them one from another as a shepherd separates the sheep from the goats, and he will place the sheep at his right hand, but the goats at the left. Then the King will say to those at his right hand, 'Come, O blessed of my Father, inherit the kingdom prepared for you from the foundation of the world; for I was hungry and you gave me food, I was thirsty and you gave me drink, I was

ABORTION, THEOLOGICALLY UNDERSTOOD

a stranger and you welcomed me, I was naked
and you clothed me, I was sick and you visited me,
I was in prison and you came to me.' Then the righteous will answer him, 'Lord, when did we see thee
hungry and feed thee, or thirsty and give thee
drink? And when did we see thee a stranger and
welcome thee, or naked and clothe thee? And
when did we see thee sick or in prison and visit
thee?' And the King will answer them, 'Truly, I say to
you, as you did it to one of the least of these my
brethren, you did it to me.' Then he will say to those
at his left hand, 'Depart from me, you cursed, into
the eternal fire prepared for the devil and his
angels; for I was hungry and you gave me no food,
I was thirsty and you gave me no drink, I was a
stranger and you did not welcome me, naked and
you did not clothe me, sick and in prison and you
did not visit me.' Then they also will answer, 'Lord,
when did we see thee hungry or thirsty or a stranger
or naked or sick or in prison, and did not minister to
thee?' Then he will answer them, 'Truly, I say to you,
as you did it not to one of the least of these, you did
it not to me.' And they will go away into eternal
punishment, but the righteous into eternal life."

"As a Christian and a woman, I find abortion a very difficult
subject to address. Even so, I believe that it is essential that the
Church face the issue of abortion in a distinctly Christian manner. Because of that, I am hereby addressing not society in general, but those of us who call ourselves Christians. I also want to
be clear that I am not addressing abortion as a legal issue. I
believe the issue, for the Church, must be framed not around
the banners of 'pro-choice' or 'pro-life,' but around God's call to
care for the least among us whom Jesus calls his sisters and
brothers.

"So, in this sermon, I will make three points. The first point is
that the gospel favors women and children. The second point is
that the customary framing of the abortion issue by both pro-
choice and pro-life groups is unbiblical because it assumes that
the woman is ultimately responsible for both herself and for any

45

child she might carry. The third point is that a Christian response must reframe the issue to focus on responsibility rather than rights."

GOSPEL, WOMEN, AND CHILDREN

"Point number one: the gospel favors women and children. The gospel is feminist. In Matthew, Mark, Luke, and John, Jesus treats women as thinking people who are worthy of respect. This was not, of course, the usual attitude of that time. In addition, it is to the women among Jesus' followers, not to the men, that he entrusts the initial proclamation of his resurrection. It is not only Jesus himself who sees the gospel making all people equal, for Saint Paul wrote, 'There is neither Jew nor Greek, there is neither slave nor free, there is neither male nor female; for you are all one in Christ Jesus' (Gal. 3:28 RSV).

"And yet, women have been oppressed through recorded history and continue to be oppressed today. So when Jesus says, 'as you did it to one of the least of these my brethren, you did it to me' (Matt. 25:40 RSV), I have to believe that Jesus includes women among 'the least of these.' Anything that helps women, therefore, helps Jesus. When Jesus says, 'as you did it to one of the least of these my brethren, you did it to me,' he is also talking about children, because children are literally 'the least of these.' Children lack the three things the world values most—power, wealth, and influence. If we concern ourselves with people who are powerless, then children should obviously be at the top of our list. One irony of the abortion debate, as it now stands in our church and society, is that it frames these two groups, women and children, as enemies of one another."

THE WOMAN ALONE

"This brings me to my second point. The usual framing of the abortion issue, by both pro-choice and pro-life groups, is unbiblical because it assumes that the woman is ultimately responsible both for herself and for any child she might carry. Why is it that women have abortions? Women I know, and those I know about, have had abortions for two basic reasons: the fear that they could not handle the financial and physical demands of the child, and the fear that having the child would destroy relationships that are important to them.

"An example of the first fear, the inability to handle the child financially or physically, is the divorced mother of two children, the younger of whom has Down syndrome. This woman recently discovered that she was pregnant. She believed abortion was wrong. However, the father of the child would not commit himself to help raise this child, and she was afraid she could not handle raising another child on her own.

"An example of the second fear, the fear of destroying relationships, is the woman who became pregnant and was told by her husband that he would leave her if she did not have an abortion. She did not want to lose her husband, so she had the abortion. Later, her husband left her anyway.

"In both of these cases, and in others I have known, the woman has had an abortion not because she was exercising her free choice but because she felt she had no choice. In each case the responsibility for caring for the child, had she had the child, would have rested squarely and solely on the woman."

REFRAMING WITH RESPONSIBILITY

"Which brings me to my third point: the Christian response to abortion must reframe the issue to focus on responsibility rather than rights. The pro-choice/pro-life debate presently pits the right of the mother to choose against the right of the fetus to live. The Christian response, on the other hand, centers on the responsibility of the whole Christian community to care for 'the least of these.'

"According to the Presbyterian Church's *Book of Order* of 1983-1985, when a person is baptized, the congregation answers this question: 'Do you, the members of this congregation, in the name of the whole Church of Christ, undertake the responsibility for the continued Christian nurture of this person, promising to be an example of the new life in Christ and to pray for him or her in this new life?' We make this promise because we know that no adult belongs to himself or herself, and that no child belongs to his or her parents, but that every person is a child of God. Because of that, every young one is our child, the church's child to care for. This is not an option. It is a responsibility.

"Let me tell you two stories about what it is like when the Church takes this responsibility seriously. The first is a story that Will Willimon, the Dean of Duke University Chapel, tells about a black church. In this church, when a teenager has a baby that she cannot care for, the church baptizes the baby and gives him/her to an older couple in the church that has the time and wisdom to raise the child. That way, says the pastor, the couple can raise the teenage mother along with the baby. 'That,' the pastor says, 'is how we do it.'

"The second story involves something that happened to a woman named Deborah. A member of her church, a divorced woman, became pregnant, and the father dropped out of the picture. The woman decided to keep the child. But as the pregnancy progressed and began to show, she became upset because she felt she could not go to church anymore. After all, here she was, a Sunday School teacher, unmarried and pregnant. So she called Deborah. Deborah told her to come to church and sit in the pew with Deborah's family, and, no matter how the church reacted, the family would support her. Well, the church rallied around when the woman's doctor told her at her six-month checkup that she owed him the remaining balance of fifteen hundred dollars by the next month; otherwise, he would not deliver the baby. The church held a baby shower and raised the money. When the time came for her to deliver, Karen was her labor coach. When the woman's mother refused to come and help after the baby was born, the church brought food and helped clean her house while she recovered from the birth. Now the woman's little girl is the child of the parish.

"This is what the Church looks like when it takes seriously its call to care for 'the least of these.' These two churches differ in certain ways: one is Methodist, the other Roman Catholic; one has a carefully planned strategy for supporting women and babies, the other simply reacted spontaneously to a particular woman and her baby. But in each case the church acted with creativity and compassion to live out the gospel.

"In our Scripture lesson today, Jesus gives a preview of the Last Judgment":

"Then the King will say to those at his right hand, 'Come O blessed of my Father, inherit the kingdom prepared for you from the foundation of the world; for I was hungry and you gave me food, I was thirsty and you gave me drink, I was a stranger and you welcomed me, I was naked and you clothed me, I was sick and you visited me, I was in prison and you came to me.' Then the righteous will answer him, 'Lord, when did we see thee hungry and feed thee, or thirsty and give thee drink? And when did we see thee a stranger and welcome thee, or naked and clothe thee? And when did we see thee sick or in prison and visit thee?' And the King will answer them, 'Truly, I say to you, as you did it to one of the least of these my brethren, you did it to me.'" (Matthew 25:34-40)

"We cannot simply throw the issue of abortion in the faces of women and say, 'You decide and you bear the consequences of your decision.' As the Church, our response to the abortion issue must be to shoulder the responsibility to care for women and children. We cannot do otherwise and still be the Church. If we close our doors in the faces of women and children, then we close our doors in the face of Christ."

AN ETHICAL COMMENTARY

I begin with this sermon because I suspect that most ministers have not preached about abortion. Most ministers have not preached about abortion because they have not had the slightest idea about how to do it in a way that would not make everyone in their congregations mad. Most ministers considering a sermon on abortion have mistakenly thought that they would have to take up the terms that are given by the wider society.

Above you have a young minister cutting through the kind of pro-choice and pro-life rhetoric that is given in the wider society. She preached a sermon on abortion that derives directly from the gospel. Her sermon is a reminder about what the Church is to be about when addressing this issue in a Christian way. That is the primary thing that I want to underline: the Church's refusal to use society's terms for the abortion debate, and the churches' willingness to take on the abortion problem as Church. This sermon suggests that abortion is not a question about the law, but about what kind of people we are to be as the Church and as Christians.

Abortion forces the Church to recognize the fallacy of a key presumption of many Christians in this society—namely, that what Christians believe about the moral life is what any right-thinking person, whether he or she is Christian or not, also believes. Again, that presumption is false. We Christians have thought that when we address the issue of abortion and when we say "we," we are talking about anybody who is a good, decent American. But that is not who "we" Christians are. If any issue is going to help us discover that, it is going to be the issue of abortion.

BEYOND RIGHTS

Christians in America are tempted to think of issues like abortion primarily in legal terms such as "rights." This is because the legal mode, as Tocqueville pointed out long ago, provides the constituting morality in liberal societies. In other words, when you live in a liberal society like ours, the fundamental problem is how you can achieve cooperative agreements between individuals who share nothing in common other than their fear of death. In liberal society the law has the function of securing such agreements. That is the reason why lawyers are to America what priests were to the medieval world. The law is our way of negotiating safe agreements between autonomous individuals who have nothing else in common other than their fear of death and their mutual desire for protection.

Therefore, rights language is fundamental in our political and moral context. In America, we oftentimes pride ourselves, as Americans, on being pragmatic people who are not ideological. But that is absolutely false. No country has ever been more theory dependent on a public philosophy than America.

Indeed I want to argue that America is the only country that has the misfortune of being founded on a philosophical mistake—namely, the notion of inalienable rights. We Christians do not believe that we have inalienable rights. That is the false presumption of Enlightenment individualism, and it opposes everything that Christians believe about what it means to be a creature. Notice that the issue is *inalienable* rights. Rights make a certain sense when they are correlative to duties and goods, but they are not inalienable. For example, when the barons protested against the king in the Magna Carta, they did so in the name of their duties to their underlings. Duties, not rights, were primary. The rights were simply ways of remembering what the duties were.

Christians, to be more specific, do not believe that we have a right to do with our bodies whatever we want. We do not believe that we have a right to our bodies because when we are baptized we become members of one another; then we can tell one another what it is that we should, and should not, do with our bodies. I had a colleague at the University of Notre Dame who taught Judaica. He was Jewish and always said that any religion that does not tell you what to do with your genitals and pots and pans cannot be interesting. That is exactly true. In the Church we tell you what you can and cannot do with your genitals. They are not your own. They are not private. That means that you cannot commit adultery. If you do, you are no longer a member of "us." Of course pots and pans are equally important.

I was recently giving a talk at a very conservative university, Houston Baptist University. Since its business school has an ethics program, I called my talk "Why Business Ethics Is a Bad Idea." When I had finished, one of the business-school people asked, "Well goodness, what then can we Christians do about business ethics?" I said, "A place to start would be the local church. It might be established that before anyone joins a Baptist church in Houston, he or she would have to declare in public what his or her annual income is." The only people whose incomes are known in The United Methodist Church today are ordained ministers. Why should we make the ministers' salaries public and not the laity's? Most people would rather tell you what they do in the bedroom than how much they make. With these things in mind, you can see how the Church is being destroyed by the privatization of individual lives, legitimated by the American ethos. If you want to know who or what is destroying the babies of this country through abortion, look at privatization, which is learned in the economic arena.

Under the veil of American privatization, we are encouraging people to believe in the same way that Andrew Carnegie believed. He thought that he had a right to his steel mills. In the same sense, people think that they have a right to their bodies. The body is then a piece of property in a capitalist sense. Unfortunately, that is antithetical to the way we Christians think that we have to share as members of the same body of Christ.

So, you cannot separate these issues. If you think that you can be very concerned about abortion and not concerned about the' privatization of American life generally, you are making a mistake. So the problem is: how should we, as Christians, think about abortion without the rights rhetoric that we have been given—right to my body, right to life, pro-choice, pro-life, and so on? In this respect, we Christians must try to make the abortion issue our issue.

LEARNING THE LANGUAGE

We must remember that the first question is not, Is abortion right or wrong? or, Is this abortion right or wrong? Rather, the first question is, Why do Christians call abortion *abortion*? And with the first question goes a second, Why do Christians think that *abortion* is a morally problematic term? To call abortion by that name is already a moral achievement. The reason why people are pro-*choice* rather than pro-*abortion* is that nobody really wants to be pro-abortion. The use of *choice* rather than *abortion* is an attempt at a linguistic transformation that tries to avoid the reality of abortion, because most people do not want to use that description. So, instead of *abortion*, another term is used, something like *termination of pregnancy*. Now, the Church can live more easily in a world with "terminated pregnancies," because in that world the Church no longer claims power, even linguistic power, over that medically described part of life; instead, doctors do.

One of the interesting cultural currents is the medicalization of abortion. It is one of the ways that the medical profession is continuing to secure power against the Church. Ordained ministers can sense this when they are in hospital situations. In a hospital today, the minister feels less power than the doctor, right?

My way of explaining medicine's power over the Church is to refer to the training of ministers and doctors. When someone goes to seminary today, he can say, "I'm not into Christology this year. I'm just into relating. After all, relating is what the ministry is really about, isn't it? Ministry is about helping people relate to one another, isn't it? So I want to take some more Clinical Pastoral Education (CPE) courses." And the seminary replies, "Go ahead and do it. Right, get your head straight, and so on." A kid can go to medical school and say, "I'm not into anatomy this year. I'm into relating. So I'd like to take a few more courses in psychology, because I need to know how to relate better to people." The medical school replies, "Who in the hell do you think you are, kid? We're not interested in your interests. You're going to take anatomy. If you don't like it, that's tough."

Now, what that shows you is that people believe incompetent physicians can hurt them. Therefore, people expect medical schools to hold their students responsible for the kind of training that's necessary to be competent physicians. On the other hand, few people believe an incompetent minister can damage their salvation. This helps you see that what people want today is not salvation, but health. And that helps you see why the medical profession has, as a matter of fact, so much power over the churches and their ministry. The medical establishment is the counter-salvation-promising group in our society today.

So, when you innocently say "termination of pregnancy," while it sounds like a neutral term, you are placing your thinking under the sway of the medical profession. In contrast to the medical profession, Christians maintain that the description "abortion" is more accurate and determinative than the description "termination of pregnancy." That is a most morally serious matter.

Morally speaking, the first issue is never what we are to do, but what we should see. Here is the way it works: You can only act in the world that you can see, and you must be taught to see by learning to say. Therefore, using the language of abortion is one way of training ourselves as Christians to see and to practice its opposite—hospitality, and particularly hospitality to children and the vulnerable. Therefore, abortion is a word that reminds us how Christians are to speak about, to envision, and to live life—and that is to be a baptizing people that is ready to welcome new life into our communities.

In that sense abortion is as much a moral description as suicide. Exactly why does a community maintain a description like suicide? Because it reminds the community of its practice of enhancing life, even under duress. The language of suicide also works as a way to remind you that even when you are in pain, even when you are sick, you have an obligation to remain with the People of God, vulnerable and yet present.

When we joined The United Methodist Church, we promised to uphold it with "our prayers, our presence, our gifts, and our service." We often think that "our presence" is the easy one. In fact, it is the hardest one. I can illustrate this by speaking about the church I belonged to in South Bend, Indiana. It was a small group of people that originally was an Evangelical United Brethren congregation. Every Sunday we had Eucharist, prayers from the congregation, and a noon meal for the neighborhood. When the usual congregation would pray, we would pray for the hungry in Ethiopia and for an end to the war in the Near East, and so on. Well, this bag lady started coming to church and she would pray things like, "Lord, I have a cold, and I would really like you to cure it." Or, "I've just had a horrible week and I'm depressed. Lord, would you please raise my spirits?" You never hear prayers like that in most of our churches. Why? Because the last thing that Christians want to do is show one another that they are vulnerable. People go to church because they are strong; they want to reinforce the presumption of strength.

One of the crucial issues here is how we learn to be a people dependent on one another. We must learn to confess that, as a hospitable people, we need one another because we are dependent on one another. The last thing that the Church wants is a bunch of autonomous, free individuals. We want people who know how to express authentic need, because that creates community.

So, the language of abortion is a reminder about the kind of community that we need to be. Abortion language reminds the Church to be ready to receive new life as Church.

THE CHURCH AS TRUE FAMILY

We, as church, are ready to be challenged by the other. This has to do with the fact that in the Church, every adult, whether single or married, is called to be parent. All Christian adults have parental responsibility because of baptism. Biology does not make parents in the Church; baptism does. Baptism makes all adult Christians parents and gives them the obligation to help introduce these children to the gospel. Listen to the baptismal vows; in them the whole Church promises to be parent. In this regard the Church reinvents the family.

The assumption here is that the first enemy of the family is the Church. When I taught a marriage course at Notre Dame, I used to read to my students a letter. It went something like this, "Our son had done well. He had gone to good schools, had gone through the military, had gotten out, had looked like he had a very promising career ahead. Unfortunately, he has joined some eastern religious sect. Now he does not want to have anything to do with us because we are people of 'the world.' He is never going to marry because now his true family is this funny group of people he associates with. We are heartsick. We do not know what to do about this." Then I would ask the class, "Who wrote this letter?" The students would guess, "Probably some family whose kid became a Moonie or a Hare Krishna." In fact, this is a compilation of a fourth-century, Roman senatorial family about their son's conversion to Christianity.

From the beginning we Christians have made singleness as valid a way of life as marriage. This is how. What it means to be the Church is to be a group of people called out of the world, and back into the world, to embody the hope of the Kingdom of God. Children are not necessary for the growth of the Kingdom, because the Church can call the stranger into its midst. That makes both singleness and marriage possible vocations. If everybody has to marry, then marriage is a terrible burden. But the Church does not believe that everybody has to marry. Even so, those who do not marry are also parents within the Church, because the Church is now the true family. The Church is a family into which children are brought and received. It is only within that context that it makes sense for the Church to say, "We are always ready to receive children." The People of God know no enemy when it comes to children.

FROM THE PRO-LIFE SIDE: WHEN LIFE BEGINS

Against the background of the Church as family, you can see that the Christian language of abortion challenges the modern tendency to reduce morality to moral dilemmas and discrete units of behavior. If that tendency is followed, you get the questions, "What is really wrong with abortion?," and "Isn't abortion a separate problem that can be settled on its own grounds?" And then you get the termination-of-pregnancy language that wants to see abortion as solely a medical problem. At the same time, you get abortion framed in a legalistic way.

When many people start talking about abortion, what is the first thing they talk about? When life begins. And why do they get into the question of when life begins? Because they think that the abortion issue is determined primarily by the claims that life is sacred and that life is never to be taken. They assume that these claims let you know how it is that you ought to think about abortion.

Well, I want to know where Christians get the notion that life is sacred. That notion seems to have no reference at all to God. Any good secularist can think life is sacred. Of course what the secularist means by the word *sacred* is interesting, but the idea that Christians are about the maintenance of some principle separate from our understanding of God is just crazy. As a matter of fact, Christians do not believe that life is sacred. I often remind my right-to-life friends that Christians took their children with them to martyrdom rather than have them raised pagan. Christians believe there is much worth dying for. We do not believe that human life is an absolute good in and of itself. Of course our desire to protect human life is part of our seeing each human being as God's creature. But that does not mean that we believe that life is an overriding good.

To say that life is an overriding good is to underwrite the modern sentimentality that there is absolutely nothing in this world for which it is worth dying. Christians know that Christianity is simply extended training in dying early. That is what we have always been about. Listen to the gospel! I know that today we use the Church primarily as a means of safety, but life in the Church should actually involve extended training in learning to die early.

When you frame the abortion issue in sacredness-of-life language, you get into intractable debates about when life begins. Notice that is an issue for legalists. For the legalists, the fundamental question becomes, How do you avoid doing the wrong thing?

In contrast, the Christian approach is not one of deciding when has life begun, but hoping that it has. We hope that human life has begun! We are not the kind of people who ask, Does human life start at the blastocyst stage, or at implantation? Instead, we are the kind of people who hope life has started, because we are ready to believe that this new life will enrich our community. We believe this not because we have sentimental views about children. Honestly, I cannot imagine anything worse than people saying that they have children because their hope for the future is in their children. You would never have children if you had them for that reason. We are able to have children because our hope is in God, who makes it possible to do the absurd thing of having children. In a world of such terrible injustice, in a world of such terrible misery, in a world that may well be about the killing of our children, having children is an extraordinary act of faith and hope. But as Christians our hope is from the God who urges us to welcome children. When children are welcomed, it is an extraordinary testimony of faith.

FROM THE PRO-CHOICE SIDE: WHEN PERSONHOOD BEGINS

On the pro-choice side you also get the abortion issue framed in a non-communitarian way. On the pro-choice side you get the question about when the fetus becomes a "person," because only persons supposedly have citizenship rights. That is the issue of Roe v. Wade.

It is odd for Christians to take this approach since we believe that we are first of all citizens of a far different kingdom than something called the United States of America. If we end up identifying personhood with the ability to reason—which, I think, finally renders all of our lives deeply problematic—then we cannot tell why it is that we ought to care for the profoundly retarded. One of the most chilling aspects of the current abortion debate in the wider society is the general acceptance, even among pro-life people, of the legitimacy of aborting severely defective children. Where do people get that idea? Where do people get the idea that severely defective children are somehow less than God's creatures? People get that idea by privileging rationality. We privilege our ability to reason. I find that unbelievable.

We must remember that as Christians we do not believe in the inherent sacredness of life or in personhood. Instead we believe that there is much for which to die. Christians do not believe that life is a right or that we have inherent dignity. Instead we believe that life is the gift of a gracious God. That is our primary Christian language regarding abortion: Life is the gift of a gracious God. As part of the giftedness of life, we believe that we ought to live in a profound awe of the other's existence, knowing that in the other we find God. So abortion is a description maintained by Christians to remind us of the kind of community we must be to sustain the practice of hospitality to new life. That is related to everything else that we do and believe.

SLIPPING DOWN THE SLOPE

There is the argument that if you let abortion start occurring for the late-developed fetus, sooner or later you cannot prohibit infanticide. Here you are entering the slippery slope argument. There is a prominent, well-respected philosopher in this country named H. Tristam Englehart who wrote a book called *Foundations of Bioethics*. In the book Englehart argues that, as far as he can see, there is absolutely no reason at all that we should not kill children up to a year and a half old, since they are not yet persons. *Foundations* is a text widely used in our universities today by people having to deal with all kinds of bioethical problems.

I have no doubt that bioethical problems exist. After all, today you can run into all kinds of anomalies. For example, in hospitals, on one side of the hall, doctors and nurses are working very hard to save a prematurely born, five-hundred-gram child— while, on the other side of the hall, they are aborting a similar child. There are many of these anomalies. There is no question that they are happening. You can build up a collection of such horror stories. But listen, people can get used to horror. Also, opposition to the horrible should not be the final, decisive ground on which Christians stand while tackling these kinds of issues. Instead, the issue is how we as a Christian community can live in positive affirmation of the kind of hospitality that will be a witness to the society we live in. That will open up a discourse that otherwise would be impossible.

One of the reasons why the Church's position about abortion has not been authentic is because the Church has not lived and witnessed as a community in a way that challenges the fundamental secular presuppositions of both the pro-life side and the pro-choice side. We are going to have to become that kind of community if our witness is to have the kind of integrity that makes a difference.

THE MALE ISSUE

When addressing abortion, we must engage the crucial question of the relationship between men and women, and thus sexual ethics. One of the things that the church has tried to do—and this is typical of the liberal social order in which we live—is to isolate the issue of abortion from the issue of sexual ethics. We cannot do that.

As the above sermon suggests, the legalization of abortion can be seen as the further abandonment of women by men. One of the cruelest things that has happened over the last few years is convincing women that Yes is as good as No. That gives great power to men, especially in societies, like ours, where men continue domination. Women's greatest power is the power of the No. This simply has to be understood. The Church has to make it clear that we understand that sexual relations are relations of power.

Unfortunately, one of the worst things that Christians have done is to underwrite romantic presuppositions about marriage. Even Christians now think that we ought to marry people simply because they are "in love." Wrong, wrong, wrong! What could being in love possibly mean? The romantic view underwrites the presumption that, because people are in love, it is therefore legitimate for them to have sexual intercourse, whether they are married or not. Contrary to this is the Church's view of marriage. Marriage, according to the Church, is the public declaration that two people have pledged to live together faithfully for a lifetime.

One of the good things about the Church's understanding of marriage is that it helps us to get a handle on making men take responsibility for their progeny. It is a great challenge for any society to get its men to take up this responsibility. As far as today's Church is concerned, we must start condemning male promiscuity. A church will not have a valid voice on abortion until it attacks male promiscuity with the ferocity it deserves. And we have got to get over being afraid of appearing prudish. Male promiscuity is nothing but the exercise of wreckless power. It is injustice. And by God we have to go after it. There is no compromise on this. Men must pay their dues. There is absolutely no backing off from that.

Christians must challenge the romanticization of sex in our society. After all, the romanticization of sex ends up with high school kids having sexual intercourse because they think they love one another. To the contrary, we must often say that that is rape. Let us be clear about it. No unattractive, fourteen-year-old woman—who is not part of the social clique of a high school, who is suddenly dated by some male, who falls all over herself with the need for approval, and who ends up in bed with him— can be said to have had anything other than rape happen to her. Let the Church speak honestly about these matters and quit pussyfooting around. Until we speak clearly on male promiscuity, we will simply continue to make the problems of teenage pregnancy and abortion female problems. Males have to be put in their place. There is no way we as a church can have an authentic voice without this clear witness.

THE "WANTED CHILD" SYNDROME

There is one other issue that I think is worth highlighting. It concerns how abortion in our society has dramatically affected the practice of having children. In discussions about abortion, one often hears that "no unwanted child ought to be born." But I can think of no greater burden than having to be a wanted child.

When I taught the marriage course at the Notre Dame, the parents of my students wanted me to teach their kids what the parents did not want them to do. The kids, on the other hand, approached the course from the perspective of whether or not they should feel guilty for what they had already done. Not wanting to privilege either approach, I started the course with the question, "What reason would you give for you or for someone else wanting to have a child?" I would get answers like,

"Well, children are fun." In that case I would ask them to think about their brothers and/or sisters. Another answer was, "Children are a hedge against loneliness." Then I recommended getting a dog. Also I would note that if they really wanted to feel lonely, they should think about someone that they had raised turning out to be a stranger. Another common student reply to my question was, "Kids are a manifestation of our love." "Well," I responded, "what happens when your love changes and you are still stuck with them?" I would get all kinds of answers like these from my students. But, in effect, these answers show that people today do not know why they are having children.

It happened three or four times that someone in the class, usually a young woman, would raise her hand and say, "I do not want to talk about this anymore." What this meant is that she knew that she was going to have children, yet she did not have the slightest idea why; and she did not want it examined. You can talk in your classes about whether God exists all semester and no one cares, because it does not seem to make any difference. But having children makes a difference, and the students are frightened that they do not know about these matters.

Then my students would come up with that one big answer that sounds good. They would say, "We want to have children in order to make the world a better place." By that, they think that they ought to have a perfect child. And then you get into the notion that you can have a child only if you have everything set—that is, if you are in a good "relationship," if you have your finances in good shape, the house, and so on. As a result, of course, we absolutely destroy our children, so to speak, because we do not know how to appreciate them or their differences.

Now who knows what we could possibly want when we "want a child"? The idea of want in that context is about as silly as the idea that we can marry the right person. That just does not happen. Wanting a child is particularly troubling as it finally results in a deep distrust of children with physical and mental handicaps. The crucial issue for us, as Christians, is what kind of people we need to be to be capable of welcoming into this world children, some of whom may be born with disablities and even die.

Too often we assume compassion means preventing suffering.

Too often we think that we ought to prevent suffering even if it means eliminating the sufferer. In the abortion debate, the Church's fundamental challenge is to challenge this ethics of compassion. There is no more fundamental issue than that. People who defend abortion defend it in the name of compassion. "We do not want any unwanted children born into the world," they say. But Christians are people who believe that any compassion that is not formed by the truthful worship of the true God cannot help being accursed. Christians must challenge the misbegotten compassion of this world. That is not going to be easy.

COMMON QUESTIONS, UNCOMMON ANSWERS

QUESTION ONE: What about abortion in American society at large? That is, in your opinion, what would be the best abortion law for our society?

HAUERWAS: The Church is not nearly at the point where it can concern itself with what kind of abortion law we should have in the United States or even in the state of North Carolina. Instead, we should start thinking about what it means for Christians to be the kind of community that can make a witness to the wider society about these matters.

Once I was giving a lecture on medical ethics at the University of Chicago Medical School. During the week before the lecture, the school's students and faculty had been discussing abortion. They had decided that, if a woman asked them to perform an abortion, they would do it because a doctor ought to do whatever a patient asks. So I said, "Let's not talk about abortion. Let's talk about suicide. Imagine that you are a doctor in the Emergency Room (E.R.) at Cook County Hospital, here on the edge of Lake Michigan. It's winter; the patient they have pulled out of the lake is cold; and he is brought to the E.R. He has a note attached to his clothing. It says: 'I've been studying the literature of suicide for the past thirty years. I now agree completely with Seneca on these matters. After careful consideration, I've decided to end my life. If I am rescued prior to my complete death, please do not resuscitate.'"

I said, "What would you do?"

"We'd try to save him, of course," they answered.

So I followed, "On what grounds? If you are going to do whatever the consumer asks you to do, you have no reason at all to save him."

So they countered, "But it's our job as doctors to save life."

And I said, "Even if that is the case, why do you have the right to impose your role, your specific duties, on this man?"

After quite a bit of argument, they decided that the way to solve this problem would be to save this man the first time he came into the E.R. The second time they would let him die.

My sense of the matter is that secular society, which assumes that you have a right to your body, has absolutely no basis for suicide prevention centers. In other words, the wider secular society has no public moral discourse about these matters.

In this kind of a setting, Christians witness to wider society, first of all, not by lobbying for a law against abortion, but by welcoming the children that the wider society does not want. Part of that witness might be to say to our pro-choice friends, "You are absolutely right. I don't think that any poor woman ought to be forced to have a child that she cannot afford. So let's work hard for an adequate child allowance in this country." That may not be entirely satisfactory, but that is one approach.

QUESTION TWO: Should the Church be creating more abortion-prevention ministries, such as homes for children?

HAUERWAS: I think that would be fine.

Let me add that I have a lot of respect for the people in Operation Rescue. However, intervention in an abortion-clinic context is so humanly painful that I'm not sure what kind of witness Christians make there. But if we go to a rescue, one of the things that I think that we ought to be ready to say to a woman considering an abortion is, "Will you come home and live with me until you have your child? And, if you want me to raise the child, I will." I think that that kind of witness would make a very powerful statement. The children's homes are good, but also I think that Christians should be the kind of people who can open our homes to a mother and her child. A lot of single people are ready to do that.

QUESTION THREE: How should the Church assist a woman who was raped and is pregnant? Where is justice, in a Niebuhrian sense, for her?

HAUERWAS: First, I am not a Niebuhrian. One of the problems with Niebuhr's account of sin is that it gets you into a lesser-of-two-evils argument. Because I am a pacifist, I do not want to entertain lesser-of-two-evils arguments. As you know, Christians are not about compromise. We are about being faithful.

Second, I do know some women who have been raped and who have had their children and become remarkable mothers. I am profoundly humbled by their witness.

Now, stop and think. Why is it that The United Methodist Church has not had much of a witness about abortion, suicide, or other such matters? We must face it: moral discourse in most of our churches is but a pale reflection of what you find in *Time* magazine. For example, when the United Methodist bishops drafted their peace pastoral, they said that most Methodist people have been pacifists or just-war people. Well that was, quite frankly, not true. I sat in on a continuing-education session at Duke right after the peace pastoral came out. I asked how many of the ministers present had heard of just-war theory prior to the pastoral. Two-thirds of the approximately one hundred ministers indicated that they had never heard of just war. The United Methodist Church has not had disciplined discourse about any of these matters.

Does our church have disciplined discourse, even about marriage? No. We let our children grow up believing that what Christians believe about marriage is the same thing that the wider society believes about marriage—that is, if you are in love with someone, you probably ought to get married. It is a crazy idea. Being in love has nothing whatsoever to do with their vocation as Christians.

When was the last time you heard of a United Methodist minister who refused to marry a couple because they were new to the congregation? People should be married within our congregations if and only if they have lived in those congregations for at least a year. After all, those getting married are making serious promises.

Furthermore, when was the last time you preached or heard a sermon on abortion? When was the last time you preached or heard a sermon on war? When was the last time you preached or heard a sermon on the kind of care we ought to give to the ill? When was the last time you preached or heard a sermon about death and dying? When was the last time you preached or heard a sermon on the political responsibilities of Christians? The problem is that we feel at a loss about how to make these kinds of matters part of the whole Church. So, in effect, our preaching betrays the Church. I do not mean to put all the blame on preaching, but ministers do have a bully pulpit that almost no one else in this society has—except for television. It is not much, but it is something. At least preachers can enliven a discourse that is not alive anywhere else, and people are hungering to be led by people of courage.

One of the deepest problems about these kinds of issues is that ministers fear their own congregations. But as the Reverend Hamilton-Poore's sermon makes clear, this kind of sermon can be preached. And people will respond to it. And it will enhance a discourse that will make possible practices that otherwise would not be there.

This brings me to comment on how we conduct our annual conferences. I think that the lack of discussion of serious theological and moral matters at annual conferences is an outrage. It is an outrage! That is the one place where the United Methodist ministry comes together every year, and yet very little serious theological and moral challenge takes place there. Annual conference today is like any other gathering of people in a business organization. Of course we have Bible study and all of that, but it is pietistic. It is pietism. It is all individualism. It is about how I can find my soul's relationship with God. But God is not just interested in our little souls. God has bigger fish to fry. If all we are interested in is our little souls, we shortchange the extraordinary adventure that the gospel calls us to be part of.

You might wonder what this means in terms of supporting a constitutional amendment on abortion. More important than that is what Christians owe our fellow participants—I do not want to use the word *citizens* because I do not believe we are citizens—in this strange society in which we find ourselves.

[*A version of this lecture was first delivered at a meeting of the Evangelical Fellowship during the North Carolina Annual Conference in June 1990. The lecture appeared later as a booklet, which was published by the Taskforce of United Methodists on Abortion and Sexuality.*]

–––––––––– Chapter 5 ––––––––––

THE MINISTRY OF A CRISIS PREGNANCY CENTER

Ruth S. Brown

Ruth S. Brown is the Director of the Taskforce of United Methodists on Abortion and Sexuality.

THE NEED AND MEETING THE NEED

I t was November 7, 1983. The offices had been furnished. Counselors had been trained. Office equipment had been installed. Now what? Did our city of approximately 50,000 really need a crisis pregnancy center? Were there, in our midst, girls and young women who were turning to abortion because they felt they had nowhere else to go?

Preliminary research had indicated a strong need for such a center. While there was no abortion facility in our city, reports of car pools taking women to another city for abortions were common and easily substantiated. A driver for a public transportation service told of taking women to abortion clinics. He said that he had not realized until later just what was going on but that he had always known the women were drastically different on the return trip. They were usually very quiet. Some had cried. Students at the high schools had spoken with concern about their friends who were seeking the abortion solution so that "no one would know." Would some of the girls and young women who were seeking abortions come to a local agency for a pregnancy test and for a talk with someone about their alternatives?

Limited advertising plus public-speaking engagements introduced the services of the new center, Sav-A-Life Wiregrass (SALW), to the city and surrounding communities. The center's initial exposure had hit a responsive chord. From the day the center opened, girls and women began coming in for help. With compassion and concern for the women who had not been told the whole truth about abortion, the center's counselors, always hopeful of finding an alternative to abortion, guided the clients toward an objective review of their present and future circumstances. Is this not a ministry that the local church might offer?

Rather than accept this role, many churches have often been collectively silent. On the "macro" level, they have viewed the crisis pregnancy problem as a "social problem," one sign that a generation lacks moral direction. On the "micro" level, they have understood a crisis pregnancy as the problem of an irresponsible, or victimized, individual. In both cases, many churches have remained silent.

There is a misconception that only those outside the Church are touched by unplanned pregnancies and abortion. As anyone who has ever worked in a crisis pregnancy center can testify, nothing could be further from the truth. Nevertheless, the prevailing attitude is that the problem is not touching the Church; therefore, the Church will not touch the problem. Sadly, the girls, the boys, the women, the men, and the families affected feel rejected by the very institution uniquely (and divinely) equipped to serve them.

Crisis pregnancy centers throughout the United States struggle daily to respond to the overwhelming circumstances of the women they serve. The centers are repeatedly challenged by not only the clients but also their families to provide individual evaluation and response. The motivating force of genuine love and concern for the welfare of the client, including her unborn child, initiates a responsive chain that brings others to the centers. In day-to-day life, the clients of Sav-A-Life, and other centers, recommend the services to friends who are themselves faced with unexpected pregnancies. The bell, which hung above the entrance of Sav-A-Life's front door, rang more and more. Each ring answered the question posed by those who doubted whether Sav-A-Life Wiregrass had a purpose: yes, there was a need for a crisis pregnancy center in our town, and Sav-A-Life was meeting that need. Today nearly two hundred women a month, often in a state of fear, come to the center looking for practical help and strong hope.

Repeatedly the question arises, "Where is the Church in all of this?" As these centers struggle to provide help for those involved in crisis, we, as the Church, applaud their selfless labor of love. In addition, from them we may gain insight into how the love of Christ is extended, in practical and supportive ways, to women, men, and their young in need.

In this present hour, we Christians should not only commend and encourage but also hear. The Church should hear the command of our Lord to let the little children come to him. The Church should acknowledge that this command from our Lord is not a call for the few who are willing to serve in a crisis pregnancy center. And it is not a Sunday school slogan reserved for children's workers at the church. This command is given to no less than the original disciples themselves. Likewise, it is given to us, Jesus' disciples of today, and it is given as much more than a challenge. It is Christ's directive for us to fulfill his purposes in our generation. We can let the children come to him only insofar as we are willing to work with him to offer them life; all the while we remember that Christ's children include the girls and women as much as the unborn children in their wombs. We must be willing and employable vessels who will constitute what the Taskforce of United Methodists on Abortion and Sexuality calls the "Sheltering Church."

CASE STUDIES

Consider the potential local church ministries which are suggested by the following case studies from the files of one crisis pregnancy center. The following profiles represent many client experiences. To protect confidentiality, all names are fictitious.

SUE

Sue was quiet, humble, and obviously distraught as she sat waiting for her counselor to return with the results of the pregnancy test, which had begun several minutes earlier. She had relayed to her counselor that she felt abortion was wrong. However, the sound of her words sounded like the words of a desperate mother mouthing that "stealing is wrong," while her children on the streets are cold and starving. The counselor told Sue, as pleasantly as possible, that the test indicated that she was pregnant.

Sue sat up and tried to act composed, but her emotions built up within her. Shortly, Sue was overcome and she began to cry. "I must have an abortion," she cried. She showed her counselor the bodily scars left by her abusive husband. "He will surely kill me when he finds out that I'm pregnant; it's not his child," Sue confessed. She then explained to her counselor that abortion would be the only logical solution. At that, the counselor asked Sue to wait alone for a minute. The counselor stepped out to ask other SALW personnel about possible alternatives that could be offered to Sue. At that time, the organization was young and had not yet developed the resources that such a problem required. The office personnel prayed together, and the counselor returned with what must have seemed meager advice. "Wait one week and see what God will provide," she said to Sue. Sue's simple, sincere spirit and her true desire to preserve the life that had been entrusted to her helped her to determine to give God that week, and others, and await direction. So it went, a week at a time, until it became apparent that Sue would have to move out of her house to avoid impending abuse from her husband.

By that time and surely by providence, Sav-A-Life had the necessary resources to help Sue move into a home that would be safe for her and for her unborn child. Soon thereafter, Sue called to inform her counselor that a precious little girl had been born. Through occasional visits she maintained her relationship with SALW for several years to share the joy of her child's growth. Her radiant smile and obvious delight in her child proclaimed the truth and trustworthiness of God's providence. This same experience could be shared by the local church willing to extend a helping hand.

BETTY

The reasons for having an abortion are legion. However, many of the reasons share a common theme: the family's economic condition is not conducive to having a child, or another child. This was Betty's situation. Betty was young, perhaps on the early side of her twenties. She came to Sav-A-Life riding her bicycle. She needed a pregnancy test. Like Sue, she soon found herself in tears when she found that she was pregnant. Both Betty and her husband, Jack, were longing for the day when they could afford the expense that comes with having children. However, their longing had ceased; Jack was unemployed.

In Betty's conversation with her counselor, she indicated that she had already discussed with Jack the possibility of pregnancy. In that discussion, they had agreed that it was not the correct time to start their family. They knew that having a child in their present condition would be a financial impossibility. Abortion seemed to be their only alternative.

Betty was absolute in her decision and felt confident that it was the best one. However, she was curious about the abortion procedure. She began to ask her counselor questions about things that she had heard from others—about how the unborn child's heart begins to beat at about the third week of the pregnancy, about how other vital organs of the body form early in pregnancy, and about how the child sucks her thumb while in her mother's womb. In the office, Betty watched a film which outlined the development of the child in the womb and explained the current procedures used in abortion clinics to "terminate a pregnancy." "Now that I have seen abortion for what it is, I cannot go through with it," Betty said as she lost the determined demeanor she had had earlier. She was thankful that she had seen the film before it was too late.

But how would Betty explain to Jack the necessity of preserving the child's life when it seemed as though they had little else to give? She left the office with some informative pamphlets, strong support from her counselor, and fortification with prayer. A couple of days later Betty returned with Jack. He had agreed that abortion was not the answer. However, up to that point, a workable solution still escaped them. Again, there was prayer and agreement among all who joined that God's will should be done and the child preserved. That evening the counselor and her husband took the young couple to dinner and talked about possible alternatives that might be available. The next day Jack was contacted about a job, and he was soon back at work. Pleased with his new position, he was elated that he and his wife could support their growing family. (Some churches have identified this economic need and now attempt to offer job-placement assistance.)

Arriving at the center one morning, a counselor saw a young girl slide something under the door and then ride away on her bicycle. It was a picture of a newborn boy. The picture was wrapped in a note which read, "You saved his life. Thank you, and thank God. Wanted you to have this picture of our new baby boy." The girl on the bicycle was Betty. Once again, the grace of God was sufficient. His love and provision prevailed over an obstacle which had been perceived as insurmountable.

LYNN

Another pressing reason for abortion is the immediate reaction of parents who try to protect their children from public embarrassment.

Every once in a while, I answer the phone and a little voice says, "Hey, Granny Ruth. I love you." It is my godchild, Ashley. A beautiful, bright, delightful three-year-old, happy and secure, basking in the love of all who make up her world. Nothing in her life now gives a hint of the turmoil present when she was in her mother's womb.

Lynn, Ashley's mother, came into Sav-A-Life, and into my life, on a Friday afternoon. Scared and uncertain, she left the center with positive test results and assurances that we were there to help her in any way that she needed help. She had stolen our hearts. She was so small for her nineteen years; so brave, yet so afraid.

On Monday, she was back with the devastating news. She needed a place to stay. Her family had not understood. They loved her, but they felt she was making a mistake. Abortion was her only answer, and she must not defy them. But Lynn could not abort her child. She had seen what abortion does to the child, and she could not allow it to happen to hers. She had nowhere to turn. The baby's father had problems of his own and denied the child was his. She had to have a place to stay. From our first meeting, I knew that she would stay with me. Christ instructs his people to respond to the stranger with hospitality. For every human need, Jesus equips his Church to respond as we let him prepare the way.

Lynn moved into the bedroom vacated when the youngest of my four sons left for college (the day before). It was quite an adjustment for both of us, but we enjoyed getting to know each other. Before long, Lynn's parents were reconciled to her decision and entered into her excited plans for the baby. After a few months, she moved back to her "family of origin" for the event of Ashley's birth. God indeed uses time to heal wounds and reestablish relationships. A very happy, excited grandmother stayed by her daughter during the delivery of this darling little girl. Even Ashley's father could not deny his daughter when he saw her. He wanted to be a part of her life, and her mother's.

It was not long until I was invited to Lynn's wedding. Now, their home is centered in Christ, whom they came to know through this experience. They are active in their church in the community where they live, for they had learned firsthand about the fellowship of believers lifting up the fallen in Christian love.

ANN

Immediate affirmation is naturally encouraging, but rare. More often, the clients leave, never to be seen again. One can only wonder about their decision. But once in a while, when least expected, God may use a life that you have touched for his purposes. A former counselor, whom we will call Alice, recently related such an occurrence.

Alice tells of her encounter with a former client:

The cashier was busily taking customer's checks at the cashier's counter where I had dined. Attractive and stylishly dressed, she fit in with the tasteful surroundings of the restaurant. I quickly gave her my check for the meal and joined my party at the door. It was after I had stepped outside and was walking toward my car that she quickly appeared at the door and called my name questioningly. I wondered what kind of mistake I had made in writing out the check that she still held in her hand. 'You're Alice?' she asked as I turned.

"What did I do?" I responded, looking at the check to see if I had signed it properly.

"You didn't do anything," she assured me. "Did you work at Sav-A-Life?"

Suddenly I remembered. A frightened fourteen-year-old

named Ann had been brought into our local crisis pregnancy center by her boyfriend's mother. The positive test results confirmed the dreaded truth of an unplanned pregnancy. Then came the desperate search for a solution. Though both knew that abortion was wrong, all kinds of pressures weighed heavily. The boyfriend, though not much older, was an honor student and planned to go to medical school. His mother appeared to be open to the possibility of adoption, but the girl, visibly scared, confided in me that she would not consider this option.

They left me that day with a great concern for what would become of them all, including the tiny, defenseless new life that had been conceived. Would such a young mother, a mere child herself, be able and willing to withstand the temptation to do the "easiest" thing? I knew there would be many to encourage her to do so; as justification, they would argue that selecting any other option would ruin her young life.

In the weeks and months ahead, Ann and I kept in touch. There were many tearful calls and battles with parents who were experiencing their own anguish. The road ahead appeared rocky indeed. And so it was, as Ann carried through with her decision to have and keep her baby. In the light of her trauma, it often seemed that all my attempts to encourage and reassure her were feeble. But amazingly, they appeared to bring comfort when comfort was most needed.

It had been years since I had seen Ann, though I had thought of her and wondered what had become of her. I must admit that, though I often prayed with and for her, my vision of her future was not altogether hopeful. I had imagined that by this time she probably had more children and perhaps survived by receiving government assistance. She would be cynical and sour on life at a young age, I had guessed.

Imagine my delightful surprise when, standing before me that night, I saw a lovely young lady who informed me that she was only one year away from obtaining her RN degree at a local college. She worked nights at the restaurant to pay expenses. She showed me a picture of her beautiful son, who was now five and obviously a great joy to his mother. As I listened to her, I heard confidence and purpose. And though not spoken in specific words, I heard gratitude.

That night, I left the restaurant feeling elated and thankful. For what Ann did not know was that I was going through a desperate time in my own life, doubting that my labor in the Lord had ever been fruitful. Ann may never know how she lifted my heavy spirit that night, but I thank her for being faithful to truth through the difficult times. I respect and admire her.

And thanks to the Lord Jesus, for once again placing encouragement in my path to recall that you make a way for your children, even in circumstances that appear to be hopeless. Lord, use me to help others experience such hope.

Alice uses the word *encouragement* to describe an encounter with a former client. Alice's present difficulties and doubts were lightened by a word from this young woman out of her past. This unexpected encounter gave her renewed hope. Most clients would use these same terms, *encouragement* and *hope*, to describe their encounters with their counselors.

SAL

Encouragement and hope are especially needed by the woman who chooses adoption. Adoption is a difficult choice for the biological mother, for not only her own natural desires to keep and raise her child are in conflict with this decision, but also she must confront a society that is more tolerant of abortion than adoption. Jane, a counselor who attended the first SALW training class and who continues in the ministry as part of the staff, has written the following account of her experience with Sal and adoption.

Sal came into the office with her mother. Both daughter and mother were full of anxiety. As Sal looked at the floor, her mother voiced her own concerns to Sal's counselor. Sal was pregnant, she was separated from her husband,

and there was a possibility the child would be biracial. Regardless of the difficulty of the circumstances that confronted Sal, she had already overcome one of the largest hurdles she would have to clear in the next few months: she had decided that abortion was not the solution. She knew that life, once created, should not be abrogated, even by the woman whose womb the child occupied. With her mother, Sal discussed having her baby, but they both knew that it would be impossible to provide a home for the child. So they came to the decision that adoption was the only viable solution.

As she continued in her pregnancy, Sal came into the office for regular visits to plan and prepare for the adoption. Sal talked much about her views on the adoption. She also relayed her inner feelings and described the changes that she sensed divine grace was making in her life. The decision to place the child for adoption was difficult for Sal and her family. Friends and some members of her family could not understand how "a real mother could give up her only child." In her heart of hearts, Sal new that, through adoption, she was giving her child a better life. I reminded Sal that, most importantly, God himself had sacrificially given his only Child.

Five years passed without word from Sal. Then one day she came to the office for a friendly visit. We talked and shared with each other the emotions that had gripped young Sal during her pregnancy. Believing that Sal was much more confident and had recovered from the ordeal of pregnancy, I asked her to answer one question as honestly as possible. Sal agreed, and after a moment of silence I asked, "Do you think that, after all these years, you did the right thing by choosing adoption for your child?" Sal looked down and pondered the question for a moment. Then, looking up and smiling assuredly, she said, "The one thing I know that I did right in my life was the decision to give up my child for adoption."

"Sal had to face more crossroads in her life, but it was clear to those who had grown close to her that she had gained maturity by facing the earlier crossroads. As she faced the joy and tragedy of life, she had a greater depth of understanding from which to draw. She knew that God could be trusted, since he had been so faithful before. As Sal continued recounting the tests that life on earth put her through, it was plain to see that many tough decisions laid ahead for her. However, it was reassuring to know that she knew from whence to draw her strength."

As Jane says, facing the difficult decisions adds strength for the next challenge. Taking wise, rather than expedient, courses of action at a crisis time in their lives, young women are better prepared to stand and face future trials. The Church—faithful to the life, death, resurrection, and teachings of Jesus—has always emphasized renewed life through sacrifice and struggle. This is the power of Christ at work in lives filled with conflict. In weakness, Christ gives strength. How desperately these women need the Church, as the family of God, as the Body of Christ, to stand with them.

AFTER THE ABORTION

For those who obtain abortions, the door must be left open. Crisis pregnancy centers and churches are not going to solve every problem. Our efforts will not always end as we would hope. But even then, God calls us to obedience through service to those in need. Abortion is deceptive, presenting itself as an easy solution to emotionally distraught women. In a radio program where several women were discussing their abortions and the ensuing strife they suffered, a woman made a remark that contained a profound truth. She said, "Satan's answers are so easy at the beginning, but so hard at the end. God's answers are hard at the beginning, but so easy at the end." In her own life, abortion had appeared to be a quick and easy fix, but quite the opposite was the reality. She had suffered years of grief before finding forgiveness and peace in Christ. The fact that she will never know her child in this life will always be with her.

At SALW, counselors are trained in post-abortion counseling to respond to the grief that often enters a present counseling situation from a previous abortion. On more than a few occasions, when speaking to groups about the ministry of SALW and the facts of abortion, I would find that someone in the audience would approach me after the presentation to talk privately about the problems they had experienced from their abortions. Some of the abortions had occurred ten or twelve years ago, but the grief remained. There are many silent, damaged women who believed the lie that abortion was an easy solution for their problem. Now, they suffer silently as they see their child in children the age that their child would have been.

One evening, as we were closing for the day, the hotline rang. It was evident from the counselor's remarks that this was a different kind of call. I heard the counselor assure the caller that she would stay, after office hours, to talk with her. It seemed the caller had no fear of pregnancy. But she desperately needed someone to talk with and had been told by a friend that the women at SALW were nice and understanding. That was the first of many meetings with Mary. The abortion that was supposed to have been so easy had left her with deep emotional scars. The only person who knew about the abortion was a friend who had had an abortion herself; she had told Mary that abortion was nothing and had recommended that solution to her. Mary was often haunted by a baby crying in the night. She could not sleep. She could not deal with the deed.

The counselor was able to help her see her need to repent— not only for the abortion but also for the sexual sin that led to the pregnancy. Then Mary was able to ask for and receive forgiveness through Christ; she was enabled to give her sorrow to him. The truth of John 8:36, "So if the Son makes you free, you will be free indeed," became real in her life.

Christ's redemptive work in this situation was not yet finished. Mary could not wait to share this good news with her friend. After hearing of Mary's conversion, the friend cried and confessed that her abortion had not been as easy as she had pretended. Mary was then able to share the love of Christ with her so that she, too, could know the power of his redeeming love. The Church is uniquely equipped to offer this healing power. As followers of Christ, all Christians have experienced this comfort of forgiveness in one way or another. It is now time for the Church to intentionally share this redeeming truth with these scarred women.

It was not unusual to receive letters from women who had had abortions. In their letters, these women expressed regret and offered their experience as a means to help others avoid the same tragedy. The following excerpt from an anonymous letter represents the collective message of many such letters:

> I . . . feel that the worst mistake that I have ever made, and the one that I cannot forgive myself for making, was in having an abortion. Even though God forgives, sometimes you cannot forgive yourself . . . Hindsight is great, but unfortunately it cannot bring back a child. The easy way often isn't [easy] in the long run. . . . I now have two children. . . . I cannot possibly describe the joy that they have brought into my life . . . It really makes me think a lot about the child who would have been my firstborn child. . . . My child would have been nine this April. I always think about the birthday parties that have never been. At all the special times such as Christmas and Easter, I really miss this child. . . . The love of a child is precious, and you can't know how precious until you have one who calls you "Mama." If this letter can prevent even one abortion, then I'm so thankful. I wish I'd never had an abortion to write to you about, but somehow I never wish it more than in April . . . when I should be planning a birthday party.

You should not be surprised to know that this letter was dated April 6.

These above composites recount just a few of the experiences of one small center in one small city. Across the nation there are hundreds of such centers that are struggling to stay open and meet the needs of women who are caught in the abortion conflict.

CALL TO CHURCH ACTION

There is no shortage of debate on the abortion issue. Yet for many, it has become a closed subject. They have come to an absolute conclusion regarding their position and refuse to discuss it further. But each day, for the thousands of women who must make decisions about their pregnancies, abortion is a nearly consuming reality. They are pressured to make an immediate choice—a choice they will live with for the rest of their lives. Over 4,000 choose abortion each day.

My seven years of service with Sav-A-Life Wiregrass allowed me to evaluate the attitudes of women, ranging in ages from eleven to fifty-plus, as they dealt with decisions about their pregnancies. I saw that, as friends and family become the major influences in decision making, personal values that favor life are often put aside. Societal pressures are also strong and appear to set the standards of decision making—economics, reputation, careers, and so on—above the concern for life. These social factors are significant factors; however, they can be addressed and negotiated by daily determination, as the above case studies indicate. Social factors do not have a finality that cannot be altered with time and effort. By contrast, abortion is final, abortion destroys, abortion is death. Abortion admits defeat by failing to deal with circumstances, by failing to find solutions.

Historically, the Church has sought the higher ground in response to compelling social issues. From the beginning the Church, however imperfectly, has sought out the oppressed and offered life in the Name of Christ. It was the first Christians who took abandoned children and provided them with homes. Opposing the practice of destroying unwanted children by the then culturally accepted method of "exposing children"—by leaving them alone in the woods to be destroyed by wild animals or inclement weather—the early Christians rescued these children and took responsibility for their care. In our time should the Church do no less?

On January 22, 1973, in the *Roe v. Wade* decision, a majority of the United States Supreme Court justices voted to strike down all state abortion law. In that crucial decision, unborn children in America lost the protection of the law. Subsequently, abortion has become, to many Americans, a rather casual means of birth control. Today, less than 5 percent of the 1.6 million abortions performed each year in the United States are hard-case abortions—that is, abortions that are justified by reason of threat to the mother's life, rape, incest, or fetal deformity. That means that approximately 95 percent of all abortions in America are performed for birth-control reasons.

Christ has not called, does not call, and will not call us to find the easy way. He calls us to find the best way—a way that offers hope, a way that offers life. As his Church, we can accept that responsibility, in part, by becoming a Church that shelters those in need. And to shelter means to lend a helping hand, offer an encouraging word, meet practical needs, and give spiritual guidance.

Christ promised that if we but have faith, mountains can be moved. The mountain of abortion can be moved by simple acts of love, kindness, and encouragement, offered by people of faith. As his Church, we can now hear his call to action and respond as one, "Here am I, send me."

A LAST WORD

Skeptics who read this essay will be tempted to conjecture that the above case studies have been embellished. They might well go on to state that there are surely many women, whose stories are not told here, who carried their children to term and thereby found themselves in devastating circumstances. To those skeptics, I hereby reply: during the seven years that I served Sav-A-Life—and since the time I departed, according to those who are still working there—not one woman, who carried her child to term, has returned to express regret about the choice she made.

By contrast, some of the women who had abortions did return to our center. They came to share their grief and seek healing. This, in and of itself, is quite amazing, for one would expect these women to fear condemnation from a pro-life center. Yet they returned to the place where they experienced the unconditional love and the true concern of their counselors. The abortion clinics, which so readily took their money and the lives of their children, were not so ready to hear of their problems. In fact, one young lady related her personal experience in seeking post-abortion help from the clinic that had willingly provided her abortion. The response of the clinic staff was, "You came here for an abortion. We did what you wanted done. Now, if you are having problems with your decision, it is your problem, not ours."

To deny the power of the Holy Spirit, who is at work in the lives of those who chose life, in order to placate a disbelieving world, would, I fear, be a form of blasphemy. Certainly, for the women who kept their children, circumstances did not suddenly become rosy. They were difficult and remained difficult. Certainly, there were, are, and always will be, obstacles to overcome. But what changed for the woman who chose to have her baby was the woman herself. Through God's grace, she found hope, she found help, and she found life.

Chapter 6

TABLE TALK:

AN ACCOUNT OF THE CONFERENCE CONVERSATION

Paul T. Stallsworth

Paul T. Stallsworth is the Pastor of the Creswell Charge of The United Methodist Church in Creswell, North Carolina.

The common calendar said it was a Monday, February 10, 1992. The Church's calendar said it was the day after the Fifth Sunday after Epiphany. The place was Edenton Street United Methodist Church, which is considered by some to be the cathedral church of the North Carolina Conference of The United Methodist Church (assuming, of course, that Methodists actually have such churches). In the Cokesbury-Isley Room at Edenton Street Church, shortly after nine in the morning, the forty or so participants were seated around a large, rectangular conference table. The conferees—laity and pastors, theology students and professors, medical doctors and church/agency staff—had gathered to deliberate on matters raised by The Durham Declaration. That is, they had gathered to discuss how the church, as church, might most faithfully respond to the problem of abortion, which has proven to be, and remains, the most durable moral-social problem in contemporary American society.

Bishop Ole Borgen, a retired United Methodist bishop, opened the conference with prayer. Praying over the gathered assembly, Bishop Borgen petitioned God for "the enlightenment and guidance of the Holy Spirit." He also prayed for the grace that would lead the conferees to "live out the consequences of our life with you and your life within us."

After offering preliminary words of greeting, the Reverend Paul T. Stallsworth, who served as moderator of the one-day conference, acknowledged and thanked those churches that had, through financial gifts, helped to make The Durham Declaration Conference possible. As the conferees were introducing themselves, one at a time, Martha Clark Boothby's reluctant admission that she is an Episcopalian drew a good-natured chuckle or two. A bit later, Dr. Edgar S. Douglas, Jr. noted that he is "an obstetrician in Greenville, North Carolina, and a lay delegate to jurisdictional conference"; then he confessed that he is "a former abortionist." Patricia O'Brien Aiken mentioned that, earlier in the day, she had been calling herself "the token Irish Catholic at the conference." But gesturing toward Bishop F. Joseph Gossman, the Roman Catholic bishop of Raleigh, she said, to the laughter of many, "But now I find that I have been upstaged."

WHAT'S GOING ON HERE?

The moderator then outlined the origins and purpose of The Durham Declaration:

"In late 1988 several United Methodists began talking, more than a little pretentiously, about how our church might benefit from a declaration, which would resemble the Barmen Declaration, on the abortion problem. [The Barmen Declaration was drafted, in large part, by theologian Karl Barth to counter Nazism's ideological threat to the faith and life of the Church during the Third Reich.] Since this talk among friends did not subside, a meeting of interested people was called in February of 1990 to begin working on such a declaration.

"The initial conversation took place at Duke University Divinity School and involved just over twenty participants. Several of those early participants, if they would but admit it, are now seated around this table. Meeting for three or four hours that day, we decided, after some debate, that the declaration would be directed solely to the church—that is, to the United

Methodist household—and not to the general society. That decision was not easily reached. Then we sketched, in the broadest terms, what should be included in a declaration on abortion addressed to United Methodists. As we sketched out the declaration, we attempted to rely upon a specifically Christian vision and vocabulary.

"Later in 1990 two editorial committees—one chaired by the Reverend Alan P. Swartz and the other chaired by the Reverend Gregory K. Jenks—submitted declaration drafts that I tried to fit together editorially. At a second meeting at Duke in September of 1990, the basic content of the declaration was approved and entitled The Durham Declaration: To United Methodists on Our Church and Abortion. During the last couple of months of 1990, the Declaration was finalized and printed. Then, early in 1991, The Durham Declaration was circulated to approximately 400 United Methodists across the country; their names had been provided by the Declaration's thirty original signatories. The 400 were asked to sign the Declaration. Then, on March 5, 1991, the Declaration was released to the press, including around 150 editors, journalists, and academics.

"The goal of The Durham Declaration is not first and foremost to affect legislative policy within The United Methodist Church, although at some point that might be one of the outcomes. Instead, the goal of the Declaration project is to affect the heart and mind of the church—her teaching, preaching, and practice. That makes The Durham Declaration hard for the greater church to understand. After all, we United Methodists are so accustomed to dealing with matters legislatively and procedurally. Some would contend that we are fixated on 'process.' In contrast, The Durham Declaration is about changing the heart and mind of The United Methodist Church. God only knows if that is happening, or if that will happen. In the meantime, we can do what we can do to attempt to be faithful, and let God take care of the finality."

WILLIMON ON THE BAPTISMAL WELCOME

When the conference was in the planning stages, the Reverend Dr. William H. Willimon had been asked to write a paper

85

on breaking the sermonic silence on abortion in The United Methodist Church. Willimon's response, entitled "The Ministry of Hospitality," suggested that the silence on abortion might be baptismally broken.

Willimon introduced his paper: "One of my continuing contentions has been that it is okay for Christians to talk like Christians and to operate within a distinctive domain of discourse that is baptismal. That has run counter to my own church, The United Methodist Church, which has been spending too much time trying to talk in terms that are understandable to people who do not share our faith, to people who are not baptized. In doing this, we have lost our distinctive vision, and we have lost an ability to say anything interesting. My paper is an attempt to discipline myself to think as a pastor—that is, evangelically, congregationally, and baptismally—about an issue like abortion.

"We used to argue that the law of belief proceeds from the law of prayer (*lex orandi, lex credendi*). So it is important to look at what we pray, and at what we say, when we are busy making Christians through baptism. I am struck by a rather unspectacular part of the baptismal rite—namely, the church's welcome of the baptized into the congregation. This is threatening to a congregation for a couple of reasons. First, the congregation does not yet know who these people are and wonders what their presence will do to the church. And second, the congregation wonders whether it really has what it takes to truly welcome these people into its family of faith. Though it is threatening to the church, this part of the baptismal rite takes on significance as a challenge to hospitality.

"It struck me, when I had finished my paper, that most of my examples were not related specifically to abortion. But that is okay, because we Methodists are not, as I see it, a single-issue people. We want to think about our whole life together."

Willimon continued: "Also, I am a member of a church that generally has not had the courage to discuss abortion, or to think creatively about it—except maybe for The Durham Declaration. Because of that, I was somewhat limited in writing the paper. So, my paper had to follow the what-if route. What if we really believed in baptism? What if we really saw ourselves as being constantly pushed by the Holy Spirit to welcome the stranger? When it comes to strangers, the unborn child is a stranger to us; in addition, that child's expectant mother is a stranger to us. And it is hard to know which one threatens us, our stability and our self-images, the most.

"As United Methodists, we like to think evangelistically. That is, we like to think about how we can proclaim the gospel to the widest array of people, and about how we can go out and baptize everybody that we can get our hands on. You know, there is much that is wrong with our church that could be cured by our becoming truly evangelistic; we would be surprised by the results."

Willimon concluded his opening remarks with this: "My paper is a pastoral invitation. We need to see abortion as a golden opportunity to repent of our sins. I like that about The Durham Declaration: it is a call to confession and repentance, which is what baptism is also about. It depicts a call to the church, presented by the stranger, to new life. It is nice that this conference is beginning practically and pastorally. That is the only way Methodists know how to think, if we think. We think practically about what kind of people we would have to be to be God's witness. That is why I like beginning with the congregation, with a bunch of people down at St. John's on the Expressway, trying to witness to a very peculiar vision about the way the world is put together."

BUT ISN'T BAPTISM A PROBLEM?

But there might be a problem here, suggested the moderator. "For within our church," he said, "there is a great deal of confusion and conflict over baptism itself. I think the latest report of the baptismal study commission deserves commendation. But the work of the commission has proven that the meaning of baptism is, ironically and strangely, a divisive problem within our community of faith. But yet you, Will, are relying on baptism to be unifying and vision-giving to the church."

Willimon replied: "In my paper I am concerned with a noncontroversial part of baptism. We may disagree about whether or not you are saved when you are baptized, about when you get the Holy Spirit, and so on. But whatever baptism is, it has to do with the church welcoming the stranger into her midst. I am amazed by that innocuous part of the service, where the congregation struggles to its feet, and says, 'In the Name of God, we welcome you.' Confronted with abortion, the church should see in the challenge to welcome the stranger a marvelous opportunity to move toward greater faithfulness than we have known in the past. A little activity like giving the right hand of fellowship and welcoming people into St. John's on the Expressway can become a kind of radical witness."

The Reverend Leicester R. Longden was the second to question Willimon: "What is the role of catechesis, or church teaching, in baptism? You talk a lot about welcoming the stranger. But in many congregations, that is part of the problem. We welcome people in baptism, but we did not do much to prepare them, to talk about the baptismal covenant's mutual accountability."

Willimon answered, "You know, we have given infant baptism a bad name through promiscuous baptism. That is, we will do it with anybody, at any time, at any place, without finding out who they are and without introducing ourselves to them. But instruction is very important." That instruction, suggested Willimon, should cover the fact that the baptized are giving up their autonomy and individuality, and becoming part of a family that is busy welcoming others.

Furthermore, said Willimon, "there are a couple of historic models of catechesis in the Church. One model was reported by Hippolytus (c. 107–c. 236) where he brags that no one is to be baptized unless she has had three years of instruction, has been checked out, and has changed her life-style. At the same time, you get Cyril (c. 315–c. 386) saying that he has all of these people in Jerusalem, gathered for Easter, who are going to be baptized and then have it explained to them later.

"Along with Cyril, we know that a lot of catechesis goes on after baptism. My paper suggests that some of the strongest catechesis that needs to take place is among those of us who already are baptized. For example, picture a young, unmarried woman who gets pregnant. Not a few in her church would probably say, 'She seems a little strange to me. I certainly do not have any responsibility to her.' To them, the church should say, 'Excuse me. We should have been more upfront about this thirty years ago, when you were baptized, but this just happens to be your sister. You have complete responsibility for her. We, as the church, exist to help remind you of that.'"

Always one to light more fires than he extinguishes, Professor Stanley Hauerwas returned the group to infant baptism: "Many in the modern age who have argued for adult baptism have argued on the grounds that you can only be baptized when you supposedly know what you are doing. In that case, baptism becomes nothing but preparation for liberal personhood. My hunch is that you get that kind of thinking when the Church is no longer in the position of Barmen. Think about it: if you were going to be baptized, and you knew that you would go to a con-centration camp for being baptized, how much catechisis would you need? You see, the reason why issues like abortion are so troubling to us, in relationship to baptism, is that baptism has become confirmation, not that you are a Christian, but that you are a good American."

Hauerwas then took a leaf from history: "The Anabaptists were not against the baptism of infants per se. Regarding infant bap-tism, their real concern was about bringing people into the Church only when the newcomers were capable of fraternal cor-rection. By doing this, the Anabaptists intended to discipline themselves in the faithful living of the Christian life; they were confronting the kinds of challenges that arise when Christians are out of synch with the way most of society lives.

"Remember, baptism is about life and death. After baptism, this kid is now ready to die. How many American parents would have their children baptized if they understood that, at the moment of baptism, their kid is ready to go to martyrdom? Holding up the baby is not this cute, little business. Baptism is about the intiation of this kid into the Kingdom of God, and that says the kid is ready to die. In that way, baptism makes a great difference in how you think about abortion. That is, as Chris-tians, as people who are ready to die by opposing the powers that are death-dealing, we are ready to bring life."

Tom Donelson followed: "When we bring that baby into the church, through baptism, the baby does not have any options. The baby does not understand the consequences of baptism. But is not the church, baptizing an infant, making a statement, as church, that this baby is part of our family? When we rise and welcome the baby, are we not in effect saying that we have adopted the baby into Christ's Church?. Then," continued Donelson, "confirmation becomes the opportunity for the young person, who was baptized as an infant, to respond more fully to what has already happened in baptism."

"But how would you, at thirteen, know what had happened to you?" Hauerwas grilled Donelson. "How would you, at forty, know what had happened to you? Baptism is the claim that, because God has done it for you, you will never fully know what has happened to you. Baptism is the claim that you should never take your own life that seriously, since your life is your life only insofar as God has given it to you."

"But somewhere along the line we, as Christians, have to personally accept the reality of God's grace," Donelson challenged Hauerwas. "Somewhere along the line, we have to come back to God and say, 'Okay, now I understand.'"

"Would you baptize the profoundly mentally handicapped?" retorted Hauerwas.

"There are also millions of others who will be disadvantaged, though not profoundly retarded. Where do you draw the line with them?" asked the Reverend William L. Oliver.

To a chorus of laughter, Hauerwas came back: "When I asked if you would baptize the profoundly mentally handicapped, it is a little like asking if you would baptize most people who teach in American universities. These are people with deeply corrupted minds, and it takes a lot of work to get them out of that situation. But seriously, discussing the mentally handicapped and baptism is a way of reminding us that, to God, all of us are profoundly mentally handicapped."

On the problem of rationality and baptism, the Reverend Dr. William C. Simpson, Jr. spoke about how adults remember their infant baptisms. Though Simpson was baptized as an infant, he indirectly recalls his baptism—the time, the place, the pastor, the church—because of his church's and his family's memory. Simpson went on: "When Baptists join this church, they often ask, 'How do you remember your infant baptism?' Well, I tell them that there are a lot of things that I do not directly remember. For example, I do not remember when I became an American citizen. But there came a time when I realized I was a citizen of this nation, and that was when I had to pay taxes. There are other things which I do not directly recall, but which are nonetheless real and carry consequences."

Bishop Borgen said, "In this discussion we need to remember the basic Methodist doctrine of prevenient grace—that Christ died for all. We have always preached full, free grace for all. The question of baptizing or not baptizing the mentally handicapped is not a Methodist question. We just do it, because Christ died for that person."

Bishop Borgen raised an additional point: "In terms of its basic thrust toward living and loving in a community of faith, Willimon's paper is marvelous. But we live that way because we believe, because we have been given new life and faith, and not because we have been given the rite of baptism. The rite is a divinely given sign, and we should practice it and teach it. But that is not the basis; the basis is faith and new life. Baptism is not necessary for salvation. Mark 16 says that if you do not believe, you will be condemned. Faith is the deciding issue, not baptism. Baptism is a means, a sign, an instrument; but Willimon nearly lets the sign, baptism, take the place of that which is signified, grace. To us Methodists, baptism is a means of grace; it is a means only insofar as it transmits something that God wants transmitted. And by the way, Wesley coined two phrases—'baptized infidels' and 'baptized heathens.' For Wesley, the question was, regardless if you are baptized or not, Are you spiritually alive, or born again, today?

"Over the years I have been very much concerned with the sacraments. In the 1960s I argued for a more sacramental church. Now I find myself pleading for the opposite, because now The United Methodist Church is on the way not only to neglecting the sacraments but also to letting the sacraments take the place of faith."

Backing up Borgen was the Reverend Carl W. Lindquist. Said Lindquist: "Recently, as I was feverishly working on a sermon about the baptism of Jesus, I referred to John Wesley's sermons, especially the one entitled 'The New Birth.' In that sermon Wesley spoke about there being many baptized gluttons and many baptized thieves. The important thing, according to Wesley, is not what is outward but what is inward. And that is the new birth. That indicates to me that, for John Wesley, baptism by water is secondary to the vast inward change that is wrought by the Holy Spirit and that is called the new birth."

Subtly engaging Borgen and Lindquist, Willimon returned to Donelson: "I like your emphasis on the church. In my church, when discussing baptism, we have focused on the recipient—that is, what age should the baptized be?—or on the parents. This shifts the focus and the responsibility off the church. But in the Great Commission, Jesus told the Church to go out and make disciples, baptizing and teaching. Infant baptism, as Stanley keeps reminding us, is a costly practice. I am not sure that my church can afford it at the present time. In infant baptism, the church is assuming incredible power over and responsibility for this young one."

Donelson, again discussing the congregation, followed: "Think about a church saying to a woman, 'We do not want to handle your problems. You have a lot of problems in your life. You are economically deprived. You are too young to be a mother. We just do not want the responsibility of helping you through your crisis.' That is, among other things, a reflection of a lack of faith."

"One of my jobs as a pastor," said Willimon, "is to push my people toward greater experiences of fidelity. I do not start out with the assumption that my people have no faith. Instead, I start out with the assumption that they are an amazingly gifted people, an amazingly gifted congregation. Even the sorriest, most pitiful, little old United Methodist church already has about everything it needs to be faithful. For instance, most United Methodist churches, in terms of demographics, have a surplus of grandparents. In terms of averages, United Methodists are older than the general population. There are a lot of older people wandering around in United Methodist churches on Sunday morning. It would be great for the church to say to them, 'The world desperately needs grandparents right now. American society has so dissolved itself that you grandparents have become a rare gift.'

"This goes along with my experience of what has happened in the black church in the South. The black church, when I was growing up, had no middle-aged people; they had all moved to Detroit to find good jobs and send money back home to the South. Then you had a church that had enough sense not to let middle-aged people raise children: the grandparents raised the children. They had the patience and experience to do that."

ABORTION IS THE ISSUE, NOT BAPTISM

While expressing appreciation for the Willimon paper, Reverend J. Malloy Owen wanted to set aside baptismal discourse and get down to another business. "I hope that the unborn child will have a chance to be born and be born again. That is why we are here," said Owen.

Agreeing with Owen, Dr. Dick Douglas contended that in Willimon's paper there is "a current of anti-abortion emotion. But the paper does not have any meat on the bone. My question is this: why are we beating around the bush? Why don't we express what we really think and ask, How are we going to stop killing babies? We are not here to discuss what baptism does for us. We are here to discuss why we, as Christians, have allowed this to happen. Why has the church not stood up and said, 'Morally, we believe that abortion is wrong'? We Methodists are confused."

The moderator replied, "One reason we United Methodists have not seen clearly on the abortion issue is that our language is so confused. Our language needs to be retrained in a specifically Christian-communal way. That is what Will, in his paper, is attempting to do with the baptismal grammar. Once we are retrained—out of rights talk and in a baptismal vocabulary—we might be able to see more clearly what the heck is going on around us. The trouble is that this approach makes it seem like we are spending too much time in school. But if we will get the language straight, that will help the church to follow through, on the abortion problem and others, in a specifically Christian way. Then we will not just wind up taking sides out there in the political arena, on the pro-life side versus the pro-choice side.

"The learning of the grammar of baptism requires patience. Also it needs to be said that what we call baptism is a great mystery, a grand mystery, into which we have been brought. But we become impatient with learning and with mystery."

"I would also stress that, at present, we have been malformed," Willimon said to Douglas. "Your sense of impatience and urgency is good. Like you, I also wonder how we got confused. One way we got confused is by using the language of rights. Recently I received a letter from a student who said he is an evangelical at Gordon-Conwell Seminary. He was asking me, 'Why are American Christians killing people in Iraq who have never heard the gospel? How did we get confused into thinking that that is not an evangelistic issue?' I think we got confused by giving our allegiance to Caesar rather than God, when allegiance to God is what baptism is trying to teach. It is a problem not only that our language, but also our whole way of life, has been corrupted."

"I am impatient," Douglas declared. "I have been in the struggle against abortion for about twenty-five years now. I am working and waiting for the killing to stop. In the meantime, lives are being lost at the rate of over 1,500,000 per year in the United States. I am impatient with that. I want our church to take a stand."

"When you introduced yourself," Willimon addressed Douglas, "you said you were a 'former abortionist.' To a pastor, that sounds kind of like conversion. It sounds like somebody got converted, somebody did a U-turn, somebody got turned upside down. Well, we call that baptism. But then you might say, 'Well, it did not feel like baptism.' To that I would say, 'We want to name it baptism. I want to call it the work of the Holy Spirit in your life, which began when you were baptized.'"

"Right. But I was baptized when I was twelve years old. My conversion did not come until I was thirty-five," Douglas said to an "amen" or two around the conference table.

"Well, it takes time, sometimes," Willimon quietly said to Douglas, as some sympathetic laughter arose. Willimon continued, "Seriously, when you are baptized, we zap you with the Holy Spirit, tell you are going to die, and promise you that your sins are washed away. It means that you are getting ready for a life full of conversions and U-turns. Dick, you are a living example of baptism."

The Reverend Thomas G. Melvin then commented that baptism is as much a mystery of life as it is a mystery of death. "The life that you entered, Dick, even though it was many years after your baptism, was growth into new life. That mystery of life involves God's love, redemption, and compassion. It is not just that we are waiting to be thrown to the lions. Rather, in baptism, we go forward into a glorious new life that seeks life, that wants to give life and not take life."

Picking up on Melvin's point was Dr. Simpson, who noted that in baptism there is a celebration of God's gift of life. He said, "In baptism we are saying, 'This is someone created in the image of God.' Yesterday, when I walked down the aisle with a baby in my arms and said to the church that we were accepting responsibility for this child, I was also saying that we were celebrating this gift of God among us. That is the part of baptism that speaks directly to the issue of abortion for me—the celebration of the reality and gift of human life."

By grace and by mystery, the moderator commented, the baptized participate in both the death and the resurrection of our Lord, according to Romans 6. In that way, as well, baptism has to do with both life and death.

To those around the conference table who seemed to focus on practice, both sacramentalists and the anti-abortion activists, Borgen issued a solemn warning: "We must make sure that praxis does not become the criterion for the Church's life. That comes from American activism. Practice needs to have some kind of criteria by which it can be judged to be appropriate or not. And that is the task of theology, appealing to the sources of Scripture, tradition, experience, and reason. I accept the importance of practice. Nevertheless, practice must be evaluated by theological and biblical reflection."

Then Dr. Michael J. Gorman brought together the concerns about baptism and abortion: "We have gotten caught up in the baptismal issue, especially as baptism is experienced by the individual. But the emphasis of Willimon's paper is on baptism as a communal event. Willimon is saying that if we, as a Christian community, took seriously our baptismal vows, if the church was being the Church, there would be options for the woman in a crisis pregnancy. There would be a community where people would be caring and hospitable to these strangers, the woman and her child."

LAW AND POLITICS

James S. Robb then shifted the direction of the conversation toward the body politic. He said: "When you talk about abortion in the United States today, you have to talk about illegitimate births. It is commonly assumed that the worst thing is to have babies from poor, uneducated, young mothers. I, too, am troubled by the rise of the number of illegitimate births in this country." Robb then mentioned an unmarried woman who was tempted by abortion because she was fearful of bringing a child into an "irregular situation."

Picking up on Robb's point about familial irregularity, Longden noted that baptismal language and practice might go a long way toward broadening the church's idea and practice of family.

Since the group seemed to be interested in putting new perspectives on the table, Reverend Powell Osteen did just that. He mentioned that Hauerwas had once written about "what kind of sex Christians are having." Osteen, who was concerned with Church teaching, continued, "We, as the church, have not worked with the believers, much less the baptized infidels, on these matters. We, as the church, have not dealt with love, sex, and how to live out baptism."

Hauerwas returned to Robb's comment: "Ask yourself, Who is producing the idea of illegitimacy? Who is creating it? It is a legal concept. It is from American law. Why should that be our concept, the church's concept?"

Kathy Rudy entered the discussion next: "If I were to get pregnant, the last place I would feel free to go would be my church. My roommate's parents go to Duke Chapel. About a year ago her dad discovered that he had a brain tumor. It took him about six months to tell the chapel congregation about the tumor. Now, how could I go to the same congregation, as a single person, and tell them that I had had sex and was pregnant? I would lose my job at the Divinity School. On the other hand, if I were in that condition, the Department of Religion at this secular university would probably throw a party for me. It would have a shower to make sure that I had enough money."

Agreeing with Hauerwas, Rudy noted that "a dominant ideology is coming from American law, but the church is carrying it. That decreases the possibility for women in the church to opt for adoption."

"There is a possibility," said Willimon, the always hopeful pastor, "that God just might use these events as a means of grace. So, someone with a brain tumor might find that, on down the line, he was in the presence of a better church than had been there earlier.

"And by the way, in sitting down with a young woman, a young couple, or an older woman to talk about abortion, I wonder if it is too difficult to remind her or them about baptism. Though Jesus talked a lot about struggle and sacrifice, I am reluctant to do much talking about that, because where is the struggle and sacrifice on my part and on the part of my church?"

The Reverend James Heidinger then focused on the abortion-and-society issue. "We have been told by an unfaithful church," he said, "that abortion, finally, is a private issue, a matter of personal choice. We, as United Methodists, have viewed abortion like that, and have been unfaithful in doing so. While the church struggles with abortion, and gets her own head straight on the problem, we still have some responsibility to the larger society, where abortion remains a pressing problem. If our church addresses abortion only as church, only internally, we are still being unfaithful. The Church has a responsibility to the larger society, which is currently in moral decay. After all, on the race issue, through the civil-rights movement, the Church played a societal role and helped to change the societal ethos."

"Jim, it is good that you put that on the table," replied Willimon. "My paper is very parochial. It is for the parish. But I am a pastor, and you should expect me to be parochial.

"When Paul Stallsworth called me about The Durham Declaration, I said, 'Paul, I am tired of our church making all of those darned statements to the political order. There is stupidity in the church making a statement to Ronald Reagan, who, if you will allow overstatement, has not been in a church in his whole life. What would he know? Do you think that he recognizes the authority of United Methodist bishops?' Paul then said, 'It won't be that kind of statement. It will be to us.' So I said, 'Then okay.'"

After speculating that both Hauerwas and Willimon make "outrageous statements that they do not really mean," and thereby drawing some laughter, Lindquist responded to Willimon: "It is easy to criticize Ronald Reagan. He had many weaknesses and failings. I am proud to say that I voted for him only once—the second time. But it is a bit ironic that, despite his churchlessness, Ronald Reagan might do more to stop the abortion slaughter, through his appointments to the United States Supreme Court, than any of the mainline Protestant churches. In fact, on abortion and other matters, he has fought, tooth and nail, against the mainline churches the whole way. It is a bit strange that this man may have done more in the anti-abortion cause than our so-called church leaders."

Letting Lindquist's statement alone, Willimon followed: "Some of you have broader public-policy interests and know a lot more about that than I do. I do not know anybody in Washington, D.C. Wondering what the church should do about abortion, I have my hands full with St. John's on the Expressway. Also I know that the wider society would be a lot more interested in us if it saw a witness, with regard to abortion, in which we had put our lives, bodies, and fortunes on the line. Failing that, it is incredibly hypocritical when we say to a woman, 'Oh dear, you are pregnant. By the way, if you abort, it is a sin. But however you handle it, it is your problem.'

"In our book *Resident Aliens* (Abingdon Press, 1989), Stanley and I refer to Jerry Falwell's save-a-baby homes. In it we said, 'Darn it. We have to listen to this man on this issue.' So the issue is not *if* we should speak to the wider society but *how* we should speak to the wider society."

Willimon also mentioned that during the days of the civil-rights movement, "the black churches provided a place where people were treated with dignity and realized their self-worth as God's created, cherished children. Nothing the wider society did could stifle that or stamp that out."

"Will, do we, as baptized Christians, have citizenship responsibilities?" the moderator inquired. "And do those citizenship responsibilities relate to the abortion problem in the general society? And as I cast my vote, should I strongly consider the abortion issue?"

"Yes, you should consider it. You should consider it very strongly. I like what Roman Catholics are doing in American politics. Catholics are proving that we Methodists do not believe in freedom of religion as much as we thought we did. We believed in freedom of religion as long as Catholics would listen to the president more than they would listen to the pope. But when there are a bunch of Catholics running loose and listening first to the pope, they get to be a nuisance, in the opinion of some.

They are not like the Mario Cuomo-type Catholics who make abortion a personal issue.

"The Church has a lot to give this world. But the big question is, How? On most ethical issues, my church has jumped too quickly to public-policy analyses. One reason for this is that if I can frame problems as public-policy issues, I can keep them away from my breakfast table and away from my communion table. Here I must admit that I am prejudiced. I believe that the paradigm for Christian political action is called 'church.' It is called, in the world's terms, 'thinking small.' On the abortion issue, we Christians have been thinking too big. Now we are putting a face on it. Now we can think small about it."

"I got into the abortion issue through politics," said Patricia Aiken of Annapolis. "I am an Irish Catholic with eight kids in our family. We thought babies were the greatest thing coming down the pike, and we still do. Well, I got pushed into running for the Maryland House of Delegates in 1973—the year of the *Roe v. Wade* decision, of all times. Politically speaking, I have always been a Democrat and a liberal. Soon after being elected to public office, I was taken out by my political cohorts and asked, 'Hey Pat, we know that you are against abortion. But if push comes to shove, when you are in the state legislature, are you going to vote pro-choice?' That very minute I had to get down deep inside. I said to them, 'No. I am sorry, but this is the way I live. If the pope said tomorrow that abortion is okay, I would be very sorry, and would think that he had lost his mind, but I would hold to my pro-life position. Abortion, for me, is not a religious issue; it is a life issue.' After that encounter with the pro-choice legislators, they never supported me. I was in the legislature for four years. During that time I had to stand up and say that I would not vote for abortion, because I think it is murder. So I lost four years later.

"You do not know how wonderful you are. Reading The Durham Declaration was like receiving manna from heaven, like rain falling on the desert. Reading it, I was in tears. A friend of mine—a former United Methodist who has become a Roman Catholic—sent it to me. My point is that you are wonderful. And the conference papers are wonderful."

Aiken then returned to political concerns: "Remember: We are all Americans. My word, how many times have we solved incredible problems together? I am a product of the Depression. I can remember how we got out of it. I also remember World War II and how, from a standing start, we saved the world from Hitler in a couple of years. Along these same lines, I have thought about abortion as a matter of public policy, and my paper 'Beyond Abortion' points to a political option that is not that hard. Having looked at this problem since 1973, I have come to realize that around 90 percent of the women who have abortions have them for economic reasons. So we could easily develop better public policy on abortion. But you will always have politicians who are hypocrites—who say, 'Do not have an abortion, it is a sin, and we will see your child years later for the draft.'"

Willimon responded to Aiken very positively, because, he said, "I am hearing somebody who is well-formed by the Church. You know, Stanley Hauerwas was once asked, 'Do you think a Christian can run for public office and be elected?' 'Yeah,' he said. 'Once.' Well, here is our example, right here." The conferees were unanimous in laughter. "I am not against working very hard on abortion in the public-policy realm. But I hate to see Christians who are less well-formed than Pat Aiken doing that."

CHURCH AND CULTURE

The Reverend Rufus Stark shifted the gears of the conference from politics to culture. He noted that American society is seriously concerned with sexual permissiveness, which is advanced by the "supersaturated fantasyland" of the sex exploiters in the media. According to Stark, it is sexual permissiveness that causes abortion statistics to mount, which in turn makes our society morally uneasy. This permissiveness comes from the radical individualism that pervades society.

"Legal sanctions against abortion," in Stark's judgment, "are not the answer. Instead, the church of which we are a part needs to get busy helping people to learn how to live in community. We need to turn American society away from sexual destructiveness and individualism. But our church's exaggerated emphasis on personal salvation as the end-all of evangelistic endeavor has reaped a whirlwind. For years we have understood conversion as a transaction between the individual and God. Such an individualistic focus results in religious practice that is highly pietistic and personal but unable to form character. Right now our churches are full of people in dysfunctioning families. But we are not doing anything about it, because we are talking about 'sweet Jesus' and individualized salvation. My relationship to God is personal, but until I have eyes to see that I must care for dysfunctioning families, inside and outside the church, then I am a charade, then I am an impostor." Stark also suggested that the church has a major interest in advancing the communal bonds of marriage and family.

"Rufus, are you satisfied with The United Methodist Church's postition, teaching, and preaching on the sexual issues facing our church and society?" asked the moderator. "Do you think that we United Methodists have taken a clearly articulated stand?"

"I think we have been agonizing over this," Stark answered. "We have not come down real hard. We have been sort of fuzzy. With regard to the 1992 General Conference, I do not hear much about family issues. I think we are woefully off track on that. We are still talking individualism."

"Rufus, your use of the word *dysfunctioning* to describe families is interestering," said the moderator. "This conference and The Durham Declaration have to do with what might be called a dysfunctioning church—that is, a church that is not willing to minister to those who are hurting, to those who are sinning, to those who are in trouble.

"Here we are concerned with the Church and how we are baptismally constituted as Church," the moderator continued. "Rufus, your critique of the pietistic individualism is right on target. There is something about the Reformation, and our fighting the battles of the Reformation, that seems antiquated. Today, if there were to be another reformation, or at least a general renewal, in American Protestantism, I do not think it would be toward the individual's appropriation of the faith—though, mind you, I would never surrender the importance of that. Instead, renewal for American Protestantism would be in the direction of the renewal of the Church. That seems to me to be the direction where the Holy Spirit is leading, not toward splintering and the individualistic reception of the faith."

Stark then recalled the account of the conversion of Cornelius in Acts. "I used to think that when Cornelius and his whole household were baptized that it was just another case of paternalism. I do not think that anymore. Evangelism is family-centered. Cornelius respected his family enough to invite it into the Church where they could hear the gospel and be baptized."

CONFESSING SINS, TELLING A STORY

Responding to Stark's exchange, Rudy followed with an illustration from American popular culture: "Magic Johnson was on television a couple of weeks ago saying that, since he has been in basketball, he had had sex with probably 2,000 women. I submit to you that if a woman got on television and said that she had had sex with 2,000 people, her statement would be received completely differently. Promiscuity today is not understood equally. Magic Johnson has been valorized in this country for his sexual activity and for contracting AIDS. He is more famous now than he ever was."

Stark offered a clarification: "But he has had to come back and say that his behavior was irresponsible sexual conduct."

To which Rudy replied, "But he said that with a smile."

Stark responded, "Well, we have got to stop smiling about it."

"But we are not going to be able to stop smiling until we recognize that men and women are now treated differently on these matters," Rudy declared.

Then Bishop Borgen spoke up: "In the church moral standards should apply equally to both genders." All seemed to agree.

Martha Clark Boothby changed the subject by asking about "the relationship between the church's compassion and judgment." That prompted Willimon to respond: "The cross, for us, gathers up compassion and judgment. My concern is that the church not make the stranger an enemy, or say to the stranger, 'This is your problem.' One of the reasons that we point to the sin of the other is that we do not want to confess our own sins. Her presence in our community is an invitation to repentance and confession."

Boothby followed: "I also see the presence of the unmarried, pregnant woman as an invitation to tell a story, a public story. In my experience, I have not seen a public space that is safe in which to tell this kind of story."

"Look at it this way," said Willimon. "A pregnant woman who

tells her story might say, 'I have no options, no way to make a living to support this child.' In evangelism, we learn that you must first listen to someone—to find out who she is and where she is—before you witness to her. And if you believe in prevenient grace, you assume that God has been busy in her life before you met her. You may also assume that she has not been aware of that action. Many times, what she considers to be failures, or big blank spaces in her life, the church would consider to be places in which God was at work. Or we might say to her, 'It is good for you to want love. It it good for you to want to contribute to the world. But we, as a church, do not affirm the way that you have sought love. We do not affirm the way that you have sought intimacy. We want to show you a different way.'

"I had an experience in the past year where the daughter's decision to keep her child provoked repentance on the part of the parents who had earlier pled with her to abort the child. The father, who ended up in my office crying, was a doctor. He said, 'God help me. I have given my whole life to help people and protect life. And then I begged my own daughter to abort her child. Right after I woke up, I went out and sold both of my Mercedes.' So I asked him, 'What does that have to do with anything?' He said, 'Well, you have to be a doctor to know.' What I want to say is that the Church believes in repentance and forgiveness, and all of that is in baptism and the cross. The doctor and I could thank the daughter for reminding both of us who we are."

Telling the story was also on Hauerwas's mind. He said, "It is terror to be a woman who has had an abortion and to be told it was just a matter of choice. Women know better than that. They know that it is not just a matter of choice. They know something serious is happening. So oftentimes there is no speech for that seriousness. There is no place for confession. So, by saying that abortion is an act of freedom, we are abandoning women. That is a part of the church's sin—we have not given people a way to tell their story."

In summing up the first phase of the discussion, Will Willimon hoped that his paper would be seen as "a call to faith, in its most explicit, parochial dimensions, which is a very Wesleyan call."

GORMAN ON THE TEXTS

Dr. Michael J. Gorman then stepped up to the microphone, so to speak, to comment on his paper. "I do not see abortion primarily as an academic issue," Gorman began. "I see abortion as a church issue. Over the last ten or fifteen years I have attempted not only to think and write about this issue theologically and historically but also to be involved as much as I have been able. Therefore, I have been involved in ministries and concerns that address the abortion issue by working in the church and in crisis pregnancy centers in various capacities. Also I have been involved with trying to bridge the gap, in my own spheres of interest and influence, between the so-called conservatives and the so-called liberals; there are many insights from both sides that all can share.

"My paper, 'Ahead to Our Past: Abortion and Christian Texts,' grows out of two concerns that I have had over the last ten years or so. The first is the neglect, especially among Protestants, of what Christians have said and done about abortion over the last 2,000 years. The second concern, which is related to the first, comes from people asking me time and time again, Why doesn't the New Testament say anything about abortion? From both of these concerns, I come to the central point of my paper, which is this: like a lot of other issues, abortion is not directly addressed by the New Testament or the Bible, but even though those texts do not speak about abortion, they do speak to abortion. Let me put the main point of my paper in one sentence: though Christian Scripture does not speak *about* abortion, it does speak *to* abortion."

Emphasizing how The Durham Declaration reflects Christian Scripture and tradition, Gorman went on to sketch the main points of his paper. Then he added: "I think the input of feminist scholarship and feminist biblical interpretation is important to this issue. Even from a feminist point of view, the Bible, when interpreted correctly, still supports the thesis of the paper and the concerns of The Durham Declaration."

Then the discussion of the Gorman paper commenced. The moderator was the first questioner: "Michael, I wonder if your paper surrenders too readily to the claim that the Bible does not speak directly about abortion. For example, there are Psalm 139 and Jeremiah 1, in which the unborn child is described in some mysterious and poetic detail. In your argument, are you too quickly setting aside such texts?"

Gorman replied in two ways: "First, although Hebrew Scripture is part of the Christian canon, my paper covers only New Testament and early Christian concerns. And second, although I personally feel that Psalm 139 does poetically portray, in very beautiful terms, that God is our Creator and that God has a personal relationship with the unborn child, I think that, academically and exegetically, there are valid scholarly concerns about how that text was originally intended to be understood." Those concerns, suggested Gorman, should guide contemporary interpreters away from reading their own perspectives into the text.

ABORTION AS VIOLENCE

Dr. Simpson then drew attention to Gorman's footnote 36 (see p. 42) which refers to abortion killing not only the life of the unborn but also the compassion of those involved. Said Simpson: "That is an important comment for the physicians who are present. Having talked, within the last week, to a couple of physicians who have stopped doing abortions, I have learned something of the spiritual and emotional effects of performing abortions."

A physician in the room, Dr. Douglas, responded: "I love this paper. I love this paper because it gives me the feeling that life is precious. That is a feeling that I did not have twenty-five years ago, when I was doing abortions. I came up with the idea that, by performing abortions, I was supporting women. I thought I had compassion for pregnant women who did not want to be pregnant; so my abiding emotion at the time was the desire to relieve them of their problems. But as I began to do more and more abortions, I began to think about the little parts of babies coming out. This began to grip me. It created another emotion in me, a remorse that, in an abortion, I was taking the life of an unborn child who did not have the opportunity to defend himself or to experience the good things of this world.

"When I came face to face with Christ, he told me that abortion was wrong. Then my compassion changed. Now when I am seeing that girl in my office, I have compassion for her and compassion for her baby at the same time. But Christ tells me that it is wrong to kill. And it is not right to compound one wrong with another wrong." Douglas explained that his conversion to Christ, to begin with, had nothing to do with abortion. "But once I accepted Christ, he later dealt with me on the abortion issue. I simply could not do abortions any longer."

"It is easy to get the feeling that denying a woman an abortion is somehow insensitive or lacking in compassion," Lindquist followed. "I think that is wrong. I think denying a woman an abortion is an act of love. It is tough love. It is not soft, sentimental stuff. It is like teaching the young people of our church that they should not have sex until marriage. Some of our young people do not want to hear that, though some do. But that needs to be said. Saying it is an act of love."

Lindquist went on to tell about countering, in a letter to the editor, a local newspaper editorial which lauded Magic Johnson. In his letter he called into moral question Johnson's sexual behavior. Lindquist later preached a sermon on the same issue and Bethany Church's response to the sermon was overwhelmingly positive.

"Carl, is your position derived from Christianity or from what are called 'traditional values'?" the moderator asked.

Lindquist replied: "I do not distinguish between Christian morality and traditional values. I believe that traditional morality is based on, and judged by, Judeo-Christianity. I do not see a distinction." Some around the table, however, did; but, for once, they were silent.

"It really is a loving thing to say, 'No, you cannot end that life,'" the Reverend Richard McClain began. "However, if we stop there, that becomes a terribly oppressive thing. If we are going to take that moral posture, then we have to accept the responsibility for dealing with a messy situation." To an unmarried pregnant woman, McClain recently claimed that her body was not hers to do with as she pleased. At the same time he realized that his body and his resources were not his to do with as he pleased. They belong to Christ, and therefore they are to be used for his sake.

"What if she had said, 'I want your money'?" Hauerwas asked.

"That was the first thing I had to deal with," McClain responded. "I have a son in college, and I have got all of this stuff like every other middle-class American has. But am I prepared to say to the woman, 'We will alter the way we live our lives to help you through this experience'? If I am not prepared to say that, then while it is true that her body is not her own, there is not a lot of credibility in my saying that to her."

It is not easy for families to take in pregnant teens, Stark instructed the group. After all, to begin with, most of these teens are deeply troubled. Therefore, the host families need training, which church agencies, like Raleigh's Methodist Home for Children, can provide. Rudy added that the churches need to offer incentives—serious incentives, like tuition grants—to the expectant to encourage her toward birth. Here, the church's message to the expectant is "give us a chance to help you," said Douglas.

ONLY THE BIBLE?

Hauerwas did not want the conference "to overlook the radicalness of Gorman's paper, which is basically an attack on the Protestant heresy of sola Scriptura [which contends that the Christian faith is defined solely by Scripture]. For that, I commend him."

As chuckles began to arise, the moderator kidded, "There he goes again."

"I am not saying that for effect. I believe it," said Hauerwas in self-defense. "One of the things that we see displayed by the abortion issue is the poor resources that Protestantism has with which to think morally and reasonably about any issue. If Protestants, when confronted by a moral problem, do not have an answer that is immediately forthcoming from what we think is the scriptural text itself, then we turn it over to individual conscience. This started with the Reformation: with sola Scriptura, individual conscience was enfranchised to think that it could read and interpret Scripture separate from formation of the reader by the Church. Insofar as the Reformation did that, it created the kind of individualism that is now eating up Protestants on issues like abortion. So, a problem for most of us is that we are not Roman Catholics, who can tell people, 'Of course you do not understand Scripture. That is because you are not attending to what the Holy Father tells you to do.'

"Our challenge as Protestants is to figure out how to argue about matters like abortion without giving special advantage to something called individual conscience. As Protestants, we do not yet know how to do that. But we cannot read issues like abortion directly out of the Scripture. So the issue becomes whether the church has been formed to have certain practices that enable us to see that we are a kind of hospitable people who want to welcome children, irrespective of the conditions under which they were conceived."

Donelson asked about the Hebrew tradition on abortion during the lifetime of Jesus of Nazareth. To answer that question, Gorman referred to the New Testament accounts of "Joseph finding out that Mary is pregnant. What options does he consider? He considers divorce, but he does not even consider the option of abortion. This is not reading into the text; neither Joseph nor the text mentions abortion. The reason is that, from the first century before Christ until the first century after Christ, Judaism said that induced abortion is murder. That was the social context. Jews historically believed that life began with breath, because of the soul-breath connection. Legally that meant that, until the head of a baby being born had reached the air, the young one could not inherit anything. However, to deliberately induce abortion, unless there was an absolute risk of death to the mother, was against the Jewish tradition."

"But then again," the Reverend Eddie Jo Jarrett reminded the conferees, "according to Jewish Scripture, if adultery was committed, the guilty woman was supposed to be stoned to death. That obviously took care of any issues about abortion."

Returning the conversation to the church and the church's interpretation of Scripture, Tom Donelson mentioned that he was raised a Roman Catholic. One of the things, he said, that attracted him to The United Methodist Church was the "Wesleyan quadrilateral," which involves Scripture understood with the assistance of Church tradition, reason, and experience. "If United Methodists employ tradition, reason, and experience in this way, are we not avoiding the *sola Scriptura* that Professor Hauerwas is attacking?" he asked.

"Whose reason, and whose experience?" Hauerwas asked. "There is no universal reason out there, unless you are an Enlightenment ideologue. And there is no universal experience

out there, unless you are an American liberal." But United
Methodists do have tradition, Hauerwas admitted, and that
includes the tradition of Judaism and the tradition of the Church
Fathers. But tradition, on its own, Hauerwas warned, is not
enough, because even "tradition has to be construed. That is the
reason why you need a magisterium—to understand the tradition. But United Methodists do not have a magisterium. We just
have one another." That, of course, is sometimes comforting and
sometimes troubling.

Simpson came next: "Somewhere—I do not know where, but
it's there—Calvin says that we read Scripture; it is fuzzy, and we
do not understand it. But then the Holy Spirit becomes like
eyeglasses that we put on so that it becomes clear to us. So,
when we are dealing with Scripture, it must be read within the
Church. The Bible is the Church's book." The Bible is more
than, he suggested, devotional material for the individual
Christian.

"Contemporary biblical scholarship is playing a role here that
we have not yet acknowledged," said the moderator. "For in
some ways, scholarship has stolen the Bible, if you will, from
the church. The church has turned the Bible over to a stable of
experts, who interpret the Scripture in a highly arrid, rationalis-
tic, Enlightenment-based way. The result of this is that the Bible
has been disempowered in the church today."

So, how do we, avoiding the pitfalls of individualized interpretation and modern scholarship, get the Bible rightly interpreted?
Donelson wanted to know. Rudy suggested that reading and
studying the Bible together in community would lead to church
interpretation.

The moderator argued that "the United Methodist bishops
might begin playing a leading role, for the benefit of the whole
church, in biblical interpretation—despite what the General
Council on Ministries is doing or not doing. Right now, they are
not playing that role. But were the church to see good, communal interpretation of the Bible coming from the bishops, the
church would be greatly enhanced."

On hearing that comment, Bishop Borgen reminded the conference that, on biblical matters, "the bishops are just as split
and divided as the rest of the church."

Simpson pushed Borgen: "You bishops are going to have to

struggle and work through these matters of biblical interpretation. Struggle and work—just as the Church has always done in council after council. At Nicea, or any of the other councils of the Church, this was never an easy task. Yes, the bishops will have to struggle and work with this. Yes, there will be division. But we have hope that the Holy Spirit will work through the bishops and the leaders of the church so that we might come to some common, communal understanding."

The Reverend Constance Roland Alt was ready to do some community-building biblical interpretation. She started by speaking about Jesus saying, "Let the children come to me." "At the time of this event," she said, "Jesus' statement was understood to declare, 'Let the little, vulnerable, unprotected people come to me.'"

As Roland talked about tradition, she drew from the Old Testament. "If the Old Testament is not replete with images that are helpful for the church approaching abortion, I do not know what is. We have the image of Exodus, where God says, 'I have heard the cries of my people. I have seen their affliction. And I will deliver them.' The people addressed there were completely powerless. They had no identity; they had no voice. Yet they were seen and chosen by the God who loves and delivers. Time and again, the Exodus motif is played out in Scripture.

"Exile is also a motif that runs throughout the entire Old Testament. Here a people has everything stripped away that was once theirs—including their land, their property rights, and their identity. But first the prophets denounced the Israelites—their destructiveness and their life-taking aggrandizement of power. Before exile, the prophets say, 'Surely, we will have hell to pay before it is all over.' Likewise, I think that the entire canon can be used, not for prooftexting, but for seeing the thematic development of God's overarching providence for his people." Roland was wisely offering a canonical approach to biblical intrepretation and the abortion problem.

Gorman was quick to say that "prooftexting from the Bible on the abortion issue, on both sides, is horrendous. I have written at some length on this. For example, Virginia Mollenkott uses Philippians 2—on Christ choosing to come down into history as a servant—as textual proof of a pro-choice position. That is absolute nonsense. The pro-life side engages in the same kind of prooftexting nonsense. But the thematic approach is much more open to possibilities. I think, for instance, of the divine feminine throughout Scripture, where God is pictured as compassionate mother." That, Gorman was saying, has implications for the Church and abortion.

TO DISCIPLINE THE CHURCH

The Reverend David A. Banks was concerned with a church's life, with regard to the Bible, prior to encountering a "crisis pregnancy." Said he, "The question is, Have we taught within the community of faith that Scripture and tradition claim our obedience? Even if the New Testament had spoken very explicitly about abortion, there would still be confusion in the contemporary church because the church today has not agreed that Scripture has any kind of a claim on us. So the issue is, Are we, as church, raising people of Christian character? What are we teaching about the claims that Scripture and tradition lay on our loyalties, allegiances, and actions? How deliberate are we going to be in using Scripture and tradition in forming communities of Christian character?"

The moderator came next: "That raises the challenge of what Professor Geoffrey Wainwright calls 'historic Christianity,' and whether The United Methodist Church will line up with historic Christianity. Michael's paper states very clearly where the Church through the ages, where historic Christianity, has stood on the abortion problem. Now, with regard to abortion, where does our church come down?"

Setting aside the denominational issues, the moderator went on to focus on the local congregation: "Now, let's get more specific. Let's say that in our local church we are teaching and preaching in continuity with historic Christianity. But, let's say, in our local church there are selected men or women who, on abortion, oppose the teachings of the Christian faith, who consider abortion to be just another matter for individual conscience. What do we do? Do we lovingly argue for the claim of authoritative Scripture and tradition? Or are we forced to throw up our hands and say that all opinions are equally valid in our community?"

Banks replied: "That is exactly the problem. There is authority beyond the individual. But The United Methodist Church is not convinced of that. Consequently, when we move into moral discourse about abortion, sexual promiscuity, or anything else, we are often left with my-opinion-is-as-good-as-your-opinion. Somehow, we must bring ourselves to see, once again, that there is authority beyond ourselves."

Then the moderator: "Were United Methodists to be faithful, would we then be able to say, 'If you believe that abortion is simply a matter for individual conscience, you thereby exclude yourself from the Church and this church, because that is not in line with the scriptural-traditional witness of the Church through the ages'? Would that be a valid part of being the Church?"

Banks followed: "When one takes the position of abortion being purely a matter of conscience, one thereby denies or misjudges the nature of the baptismal community." After all, at baptism, "who I am as a Christian, in the community of faith, becomes more significant than who I am as an American, or who I am as a white male. If some in the church claim that abortion is just a private issue, the church must tell them that they are not understanding how formative the gospel is for our identity."

"The abortion-is-an-issue-of-individual-conscience position works like an acid on the church," said Stallsworth. And that acid requires remedy, he went on to imply. "While serving a church, Greg Jenks once went to a parishoner and said, 'Sir, you can continue your relationship with the Ku Klux Klan and leave The United Methodist Church, or you can discontinue your relationship with the Klan and stay a United Methodist.' At some point, is our church going to have to exert similar discipline with regard to abortion?"

Lindquist questioned this line of questioning: "You can do that with the Klan, because there is a consensus in our church that the Klan is outside the boundaries of our church. However, on abortion our church is now deeply divided. Our church, like others, is at war, ideologically, over this issue. For our church, it is a civil war. In that regard, The United Methodist Church is not a community. In fact, on abortion, a majority of our church's leadership probably stands against what those of us around this table stand for. Given these realities, to declare that anybody who is pro-choice is beyond the pale is to write ourselves out of the church." All that can be done in the meantime, said Lindquist, is to "do battle" in behalf of the unborn and their mothers.

"Fundamentally, the church struggle today," the moderator claimed, "is over whether we are going to be the Church, or whether we are just going to be collections of individuals who happen to worship together every Sunday morning. The abortion issue lights up this struggle."

Rudy wanted Methodism to think harder about a pro-choice versus pro-life dialogue. "That conversation needs to happen in our church." After all, said Rudy, our church is spending money that, in effect, supports pro-choice political forces. "That same money could be going to support women who are trying to have children," she argued, and our church needs to talk about that.

Malloy Owen spoke next: "Nothing would more disqualify us from participating in the dialogue that Kathy wants than for us to say, 'The time will come when we will rule out of the church anyone who does not agree with us.' That confirms the worst fears of those who disagree with us, and casts us in the lot of unreasonable zealots."

"At this stage in the game, you are right, Malloy," said the moderator, who went on to bring up a hypothetical case drawn from the partisan-political realm. "What if David Duke, the Louisiana politician, who panders to racists and anti-Semites, were a United Methodist? By advancing racist and anti-Semitic politics, would Duke exclude himself from The United Methodist Church?"

Owen was quick to respond: "Because of the general openness and permissiveness of The United Methodist Church, as we have known it, that would be an uncharacteristic departure from what we have become and what we are. It would be a radical thing for us to exclude anyone, for any reason, from our membership. Here we are probably wrong, but I cannot imagine our church throwing out Duke or anyone else for any crime that they would commit. We just do not practice excommunication. Perhaps it is unfortunate that we do not. But that is what we have become."

"But Duke, in this example, excludes himself from the church," stated the Reverend Bill Presnell. "That is where we need to come down. Yes, there is a church standard. And you exclude yourself from the church when you do not adhere to the standards of the church. We need to say that sin is sin. We are not saying that you are excluded because you are a sinner, but that, by continuing in sin and by rationalizing sin, you are excluding yourself."

Douglas insisted that the church should not change its standards for the sake of inclusivity. "Our church would be stronger and have more credibility in the world if we stood up and said something, rather than being milquetoast about it," he said. "Take for an example the problem of homosexuality. The church loves and affirms homosexuals; but the church also holds them accountable to a standard. The church has to take a stand." Douglas spoke about loving those in error into the church's belief and way of life, but not letting them change the church's standard.

"Dick, is there a point at which tough love is necessary?" asked the moderator. "For example, think about an unrepentant abortionist, who is a church member and who continues his practice, who thinks that his work is within the boundaries of the Christian faith and is justifiable. Is there a time when the church approaches the abortionist and says, 'Your abortion practice is excluding you from participation in our community.'"

"Scripturally, I think that that would be correct," said Douglas.

Bishop Borgen qualified, "When somebody falls, we should remember the spirit of Scripture. The church should go to that person to admonish and to guide—in love, not in a judgmental or legalistic way. Then, if that person is unrepentant, the church says to that person, 'Your actions have excluded you from the spiritual community.'" This distinguishes between the person and the sin.

"When we talk about the Church," the bishop continued, "we must remember that we are not talking about just another sociological institution. We are talking about the Body of Christ, and the Body of Christ is not bound together just by being a community, or by being together in the same place or in the same way. The Body of Christ is gathered and bound together by the love of God, by the Holy Spirit, by God's peace and love. If love is absent, even in an organized Christian church, then I do not think that it is the Body of Christ, though it might claim to be. If love is absent from a church, then that church has not lived out what it is supposed to be."

The Reverend Gregory Jenks picked up where Borgen left off. Like Borgen, he was concerned with the healing, restoration, and redemption which motivate and direct church discipline. "The problem," Jenks carried on, "with the so-called mainline Protestant churches is that we have failed to say that there is anything wrong with abortion. Because we have not said that, we have not been able to offer healing to the women and men whose lives are in need of that healing. In my experiences within the pro-life community, the fundamentalist churches have most readily offered healing to women who have aborted. The number of women who have had abortions in Operation Rescue is unbelievable. Our silence, in The United Methodist Church, has been under the guise of compassion. But our silence has withheld healing. Therefore, women and men involved in abortion have had to look elsewhere for healing and redemption."

Jarrett then suggested that, regarding abortion, the church sidestep the issue of discipline and just return to its historic works of mercy. Why not follow the example of the early Christians who took in children, who had been abandoned to die, and reared them in the faith? she asked.

But that kind of ministry was connected with "a community that knew what she thought about abortion," the moderator asserted. "The church of the Roman Empire was not a church that said, 'Come on out and join us, no matter what your position on abortion.' The church of the Roman Empire was a clearly defined community that knew precisely what the compassionate, disciplined Christian life looks like."

The Reverend Pat Tony spoke next: "When our churches say No to ministry to the least of these, we become the poorer for it. When we say the Yes that the cross requires, we have the opportunity to be a real church and to have the authority of Jesus Christ." In the Church formed by its Head, Jesus Christ, sacrifice and service, Tony was saying, are tied in with authority.

A DEATH-DEALING SOCIETY

Pointing to Gorman's use of the phrase "directorate of death," Hauerwas changed the subject. "One thing that we left out of

The Durham Declaration," Hauerwas said, "is an acknowledgment that we are a part of a directorate of death. That is a name for our society, even though many of us persist in thinking our society is some kind of Christendom. But notice that Gorman's texts do not think about abortion in terms of individual will; they think about abortion in terms of a battleground of powers that we do not control. What God has given to us is the gift of being called out from some of those powers to live a different kind of life that will make those powers hate you.

"One of the troubles with this approach is that it seems you have to deal with all moral problems before you deal with an issue like abortion. Even so, you cannot ignore the fact that most of the Christian churches in this country put yellow ribbons on their doors during the Persian Gulf War. Even if it was a just war, just warriors never ask to be celebrated. For Christians, this is mournful, mournful, mournful! You cannot ignore the fact that we Christians are under a directorate of death but that we are life people. Abortion and war are not separable matters. You cannot read the early Christian texts, and think that these matters are separable." Look at the way the United States tried to handle Saddam Hussein, Hauerwas challenged, to be reminded that American society is under a death directorate.

"But the rightful role of government is to protect the innocent and punish the guilty," said James Robb. "In the case of Saddam Hussein, we cannot nurture him. We have to punish him."

"Who is the 'we'?" Hauerwas asked.

"Well, we are citizens of the city of God and the city of man at the same time," Robb replied.

"That is your problem," Hauerwas came back.

"But that represents Saint Augustine and 1600 years of Christian tradition," argued Robb.

"But that has been wrong," Hauerwas curtly but unsatisfactorily responded, to much laughter.

Gorman topped off the discussion of his paper. "The difficulty with the abortion issue in The United Methodist Church is underlined by the fact that the Religious Coalition for Abortion Rights rents space in the Methodist Building in Washington, D.C. No pronouncement from us is going to change that. We have some very serious work ahead of us.

"Futhermore, I believe that you can argue definitively that all the writers of the New Testament, if you could ask them, would have opposed abortion. After all, all the writers, except for Luke, were Jews," and the Jewish community, as Gorman had argued, was staunchly opposed to abortion.

HAUERWAS VERSUS CONVENTIONAL WISDOMS

Stanley Hauerwas began by noting that his paper was derived from a lecture that he had delivered at the North Carolina Annual Conference in June of 1990. He carried on: "Years ago, as a typical United Methodist, I had never thought about the so-called problem of abortion. I got to thinking about it because I was lucky enough to be asked to work with the mentally handicapped while I was teaching at Notre Dame. That is when I got to thinking about the presuppositions of our lives that make it possible to welcome mentally handicapped people—both those who are genetically handicapped and those who are environmentally handicapped—among us. The question was, What kind of people do we have to be to be hospitable to the mentally handicapped? That is the context in which I started thinking about abortion. That is the context where it became clear to me that, if you are a member of the Church of Jesus Christ, then you need to be open, whether you are married or not, to the responsibilities of children."

Hawerwas continued with the big picture: "American society is the first society that the world has known in which the state had to be founded first so that the social order had time to develop. As a result, American society is the most statist society in the world, though we like to think that we have a limited government. That is why bureaucratic capitalism is our social order." In this setting, ethics and politics aim only to secure cooperation among people who share very little in common; ethics and politics have to do with establishing rules and procedures of fair play, according to Hauerwas.

"Justice therefore becomes," he said, "those principles that create institutions and procedures for distributing the greatest good to the greatest number of citizens, irrespective of who they are. Contrary to that is the classical view, which assumes that justice has to do with people being just, prior to the social order being just. For example, according to Aristotle, a person was unjust if he refused to demand an honor that was due him." What American society does is separate "virtues we should have as people from the social organizations we develop. This is where we get the split between private life and public life.

"All my work on abortion is based on this premise: you cannot separate the act called abortion from the kind of people and virtues that create that description of that action. For the Church, abortion is a description with which we remind ourselves of the virtues we should have as a Christian people—and that especially includes the virtue of hospitality, the readiness to welcome new life among us, to the point of challenging the way we live. When Christians say, 'There was an abortion in our community,' they are bringing judgment upon the Church. For their comment raises the question, How could this possibly happen among us, a people that is ready to be hospitable to one another and to the stranger?"

Sooner or later the question comes up, Hauerwas conjectured, "How does the Church relate to the wider society that is not formed by the Church's virtues?" The answer is, 'Like porcupines make love, and that is very carefully.' The Church does not translate its message directly into the language of the wider society. Instead, the Church witnesses with its own language. What we have to give to the wider society is, first and foremost, our witness—which includes who we are, what we say, and what we do."

LIFE IS NOT SACRED?

Gorman was Hauerwas's first questioner, "Stan, if life, as you say, is not an overriding good, and if there is, as you say, much to die for, then there must be some things worth killing for. How would you prevent someone from drawing that conclusion?"

"There is no way to prevent that," said Hauerwas. "No people have been as enthusiastic about killing as Christians have been. Why is this so? Because for so many centuries Christians were so enthusiastic about dying. It is easy to make the transition between a willingness to die and a willingness to kill in order to protect.

"But Jesus will not let us kill," Hauerwas said. "Therefore, I am a pacifist. And all of you in this room are pacifists too. Some of you may be just-war people. But insofar as you are a just-war person, and insofar as you believe that the use of violence by Christians is an extraordinary thing that occurs only under certain conditions, then you are a pacifist. Otherwise, you believe that violence is all there is, and you are just a political realist.

"My problem with the life-is-sacred argument is that it is Promethean idolatry to believe that God always wants to protect life, as an end in itself, in and of itself. Several years back when we were discussing nuclear war, some would say, 'Oh my goodness! Nuclear weapons threaten to destroy the human species and therefore they are very, very bad things.' To that, I said that we needed to remember that God intends that we all die in the end. The problem with nuclear weapons is not that they can destroy the human species; the problem, for the Church, is murder. As Christians, we would rather that the human species be destroyed than that we commit murder. So, I do not want to say that life is inherently sacred, but that God gives us life, through which we then acknowledge it as sacred only because it is God's gift. But we do not consider life, in and of itself, sacred."

THOSE HARD CASES

On those occasions when United Methodists discuss abortion, the "hard cases"—that is, pregnancies that result from rape or incest, that threaten the life of the mother, and that involve a severely deformed unborn child—are oftentimes first discussed. Applying the general thrust of The Durham Declaration to the hard cases, Hauerwas noted that, when confronted with a hard-case pregnancy, Christians should not ask, How can I get out of this in the easiest way? Rather, when confronted with a woman who is pregnant due to rape, for example, Christians ask, "How can we help you deal with this?" and "Is abortion really the primary way to deal with this?"

Hauerwas went on to explain, "There is the famous illustration by Judith Jarvis Thompson that has become an analogy, for many people, on the hard cases. It goes like this. You wake up one morning, and you find yourself medically hooked up to a person whom you have not met before. He is a famous violinist, who has a rare disease that is possibly operable in nine months. The Violinist Society of America found out, through a computer bank and blood typing, that you could save this man for the next nine months. Otherwise, the violinist would die immediately. So a drug was slipped into your coffee, and you went to sleep and were hooked up to the violinist. Now, your blood is constantly flowing through the violinist and will continue to do so for nine months. So, you wake up and say, 'Hey, this is awful! I did not agree to this! Unhook me!' But the medical people say, 'If we unhook you, you will kill the violinist. Do you want to kill the violinist? That is terrible! Therefore, we are going to keep you hooked up to the violinist for the next nine months. You can voluntarily make this a good, sacrificial thing by keeping the violinist going.'

"What Judith Jarvis Thompson attempts to do with this example is to help us think about what it would be like to be a woman who has been raped, is pregnant, and is having to keep her oppressor's child. It would be extraordinary for this woman to say, 'This was meant for evil, but God has given me good in it.' That might be a wonderful thing to do. But as the Christian community, do we say, 'That is absolutely the way you must respond'? If you want to say that, you need to see the implications for how your community would have to be shaped. Your community would have to be shaped in ways that would make rape less likely, even though pregnancy by rape will eventually happen in it, and in ways that would prepare the community for the hard cases."

Then Hauerwas reminded the conferees that, in the Church, there are always parents—biological or not—who are ready to receive children. So, with regard to pregnancy by rape, a church can say "this is a terrible, oppressive context in which abortion might be reasonably and tragically contemplated." On the other hand, "the church can say to a woman who has been raped, 'We think it might be good for you to have this child.' That is extraordinary. But we can say that only if we are the kind of community that is ready to bear such burdens."

Taking up another of the hard cases, Kathy Rudy mentioned that a very high percentage of unborn children who have been discovered by amniocentesis to have Down syndrome are now aborted. To that, Hauerwas "could not imagine how the fact that a child has Down syndrome would make a difference for Christians. That also means that you do not put pressure on your medical professionals to develop technologies that will allow you then to search and destroy. Also, consider the technologies that, when applied to the unborn, can assist them. For example, because of medical advances, you can significantly affect the extent of an unborn child's retardation by changing the diet of the mother. That is not unimportant. I am not against that. I am not a medical Luddite. But we must remember that technologies always come with institutional purposes that should be examined.

"We must also remember that today compassion is often about eliminating the sufferer. We do not like to have sufferers among us. So, in our contemporary social situation, I am very suspicious of what is called compassion."

THINKING ABOUT DOCTORING

At the urging of Lindquist, Hauerwas reflected on the American medical establishment. First came the good news: "When people ask me where there are schools of virtue, I say Parris Island and medical school, and I am serious about that. In medical school, young physicians are schooled out of taking themselves seriously, for the sake of the care of their patients. For example, physicians are always taught that their primary obligation is to the patients in front of them, in a way that overrides all other moral considerations. That is wonderful moral formation. The patient may be a crass, child-molesting murderer, but if he has a bad gall bladder, the physician is obligated to take care of him. That takes extraordinary moral commitment. So medicine is one place in American society where moral discourse remains alive. Physicians may not know it, but they form a powerful moral community."

But then came the bad news about American medicine. Said the Duke ethicist, "Regarding salvation, if today's church really wants to see who its competitor in this world is, it should look at Duke Medical Center. Look at it this way. During the Middle Ages people would go around looking at cathedrals and think that that was a worthwhile thing to do. Today people no longer go to cathedrals. They go to Duke Medical Center, with a similar kind of awe. In the future, people will go through our hospitals and say, 'Look at those operating rooms. Man, death really must have scared the hell out of those Americans who lived late in the twentieth century.' I am not saying that just to be critical of medicine, because our society gets the kind of medicine that it deserves and wants.

"Unfortunately, medicine is increasingly susceptible to consumer demand. It is now getting to the point where the physician must do exactly what the patient/consumer wants. Think about it: why should breast enlargement be a medical problem? In this instance and many others, medicine is having difficulty resisting capitalization. Indeed medicine is becoming part of the market. Most people call that freedom. I do not."

Hauerwas then told of being with a group of doctors in an in-vitro-fertilization clinic. "One of the doctors said, 'We have a problem with abortion.' So I said, 'Oh really? What is it?' He said, 'Well, sometimes we get multiple conceptions. If we get four or five, then we have to take out two or three of them. That is very unaesthetic.' I said, 'Unaesthetic. Now that is a very interesting description. Couldn't you just say that it is wrong?' 'No,' he said, 'we are in the baby-making business here, and that is just unpleasant. Of course, there is nothing wrong with abortion. I just got back from aborting a fetus with Down syndrome.' So I asked, 'Why did you abort the fetus with Down syndrome?' 'Well,' he said, 'you know, they are just pets.' So I said, 'I have some parents that I would like you to talk to.' Then he said, 'Let's not talk about this. It is too controversial and too emotional. Let's talk about the problem of selection.' I said, 'Okay.' He said, 'We have a real problem. We cannot turn down single women who want our services.' 'Why is that a problem?' I asked. He said, 'Well, we are not too sure about parental presuppositions.' I said, 'But there are ways of getting pregnant other than going to a fertility clinic.' He said, 'Some women are too unsure of the males they might meet. They want to be able to select the sperm in a carefully controlled circumstance.' So I said, 'Consider a lady who said that she wants to have only a girl. If the child turns out to be a boy, she will abort. She is a radical feminist, and she wants to raise her daughter to be an in-vitro-fertilization therapist in order ultimately to eliminate males. Would you impregnate her?' 'No,' he said. 'Why?' I asked. 'Because heterosexual intercourse is written into DNA molecules.' So I said, 'You have got to be kidding. Only Catholics think that they can read the physical that carefully.'

"This was a real conversation. Then three other doctors in the clinic said they would do it. See, with these doctors, you are looking at guys playing with a new toy, and they do not know what in the hell they are doing. They are getting no moral direction."

Even though they have little direction, American physicians do have abundant power, argued Hauerwas. "They are becoming the new Roman Catholic Church. Who do you want to run your life—the guys in black, or the guys in white?" The laughter around the table was cranking up again, as Hauerwas went on: "As soon as you turn any problem—for example, abortion—into a medical problem, you increase the power of the medical profession. You have to run to the doctor and say, 'Oh doc, what should I do?,' and the doctor tells you. People used to act toward priests the way they now act toward their doctors, I used to tell the priests at Notre Dame. If the doctor says to you, 'Here, take three of these every three hours,' you do it, and you do not even ask why. You have come under the power of professional dominance, because you think that it is going to save you. So, one of the unspoken stories about abortion in our society is that it is a battle for turf between the Church and the medical profession. Because of this, if you are pro-choice, you are more likely than not pro-doctor."

Hauerwas also argued that death in America had been medicalized as well. Today, he said, "we want to die suddenly and without pain. No last unction among us, right? Then comes the demand for euthanasia, because of our presumptions that we are living too long. Today people just do not know how to die."

"So, we are saying that the doctor is the last refuge of morality, but society has corrupted him," Donelson summarized, and Hauerwas agreed.

If the medical establishment has tried to make abortion its problem, the legal establishment, using the language of rights and attempting to delineate when "personhood" begins, has tried to do the same thing. Opposed to these approaches is Caroline Whitbeck, a Quaker philosopher who teaches at the Massachusetts Institute of Technology. She approaches matters like abortion by asking, said Hauerwas, "'How do I feel when I am pregnant? How do I feel when I have a miscarriage?' She just wants to know. Those questions are more powerful approaches to abortion than the usual principles that are referred to."

"Should we Christians take a totally agnostic position on whether the fetus is human life or not?" asked the Reverend Mathew Woodley.

"No," Hauerwas replied quickly. "The fetus is not a cabbage. Given the kind of community we are, we always hope. If conception occurs, we are going to rejoice in the life. That is part of the way we have been trained to be.

"In interviews of women that will have abortions, most do not use the language of pro-choice or pro-life. They say, 'I would have this *baby* if my lover wanted her.' That is what they say. They do not say, 'This is just a piece of flesh.' They understand the great tragedy that is about to happen."

THE FAMILY QUESTIONED

Stark quizzed Hauerwas on the place of the family in the Church. With characteristic directness, Hauerwas responded by contending that "the Church looks on the family with great suspicion. After all, the family can be a hell hole of alternative salvation. Roman Catholics use the language of the family as a 'domestic church.' That is terrrible, because the Church alone has the ability to save. The Church stands over against the family to remind the family that it is not the primary carrier of the gospel of Christ. The Church is.

"People forget that the Church destroyed the Roman family. Christians did that because we said, 'That is not who we are. We do want to be making children for Caesar.'" Nor should Christians raise children simply to be happy and successful in the world. "We Christians," Hauerwas went on, "are destroying our kids because we think that they are supposed to have a happy life. But they are Christians! How can they have a happy life? They might go to Duke, and they might even survive that as Christians. But that is not going to be easy."

All baptized adults in the Church—both those who are married and those who are single—are baptismally charged to be parents, according to Hauerwas. Their parenting is based on and aims toward the common thought and practice of their primary community, the Church. On that point, Hauerwas, the Texan, drew a story from his past: "When I was a kid, I got a BB gun when I was ten, of course. A Roy Rogers model. The only thing I could hit with my gun was Mrs. Hargrove's watermelons. But I had no idea that, if you shot a watermelon with a BB, it would shrivel. Well, when Mrs. Hargrove saw me shoot some of her watermelons, she came over to my house and beat the hell out of me for it. It never occurred to Mrs. Hargrove to ask my mother and father whether that was appropriate. We all knew that we should not shoot up other people's watermelons with BB guns. Likewise, the Church is that community of people, with agreed-upon goods about parenting one another's children.

"Our biological children are not really our children. Think about the extraordinary possessiveness that the phrase 'our children' suggests. As a pacifist, I find people asking me, 'What happens when somebody breaks into your house and threatens to kill your wife and your child?' I say, 'Well, to begin with, they are not mine. They are God's. As members of a community called Church, they would rather die than for me to kill.'"

Possessiveness can also go the other way, Willimon warned. "My wife's father was a Methodist minister," he said. "She always felt bad that her father did not have a lot of time to spend with his children. He was always off with everybody else's children. His attitude to his children was, we will take you to church and expose you to Sunday school teachers and others. Later in life, my wife was able to see that that was a great gift for her parents to give her—the knowledge that she was not the most important project in their lives. Other people had claims upon them, and they were trying to be faithful to them.

"We may be among some of the first to ask such absurdly unrealistic things of marriage. I frequently meet a couple who will say that they could not possibly get married and have this child, because they do not have their cars paid for, are still renting, and so on. Or they will say that they just do not love each other. To that, I say, 'Don't worry about that. We will not ask you about that in the service when we marry you.'"

Willimon then noted that Stark's litany of social pathologies, which he had spun out earlier in the day, is a gracious invitation by God for us to say, "We never have had much faith in the institutions that the Romans put so much faith in. We Christians believe in a tribe, in a larger assembly," than the family. And that tribe, of course, is the Church.

CIRCLING THE WAGONS?

Les Longden, and others, suggested that some of the ideas in the conference air at that particular juncture might be considered quite alien to most United Methodists. Indeed, to several, some of the ideas seemed downright sectarian and seemed to imply withdrawal from the general society. To that, Hauerwas replied, "We are sitting here at Edenton Street United Methodist Church in Raleigh. This does not look like withdrawal to me. The problem is that, in the church today, we do not fear people who are not Christians. We tend to fear other Christians."

"When I read your *Resident Aliens*, said Lindquist to Hauerwas and Willimon, "I felt schizophrenic, in the popular sense of that word. I really like part of what you are saying. I like the part where you talk about the church being the Church, living up to what we are supposed to be, and not letting the world set our agenda. But the other side of me gets infuriated. When I read your books, I start kicking things at home, because of your fairly absolute rejection of our culture and our society.

"I am conservative—in both political philosophy and theology. The America that you portray is not the America that I know. As I read you, you seem to want to reject every part of our experience as a nation. I, too, find a lot that is wrong with our country and our culture. That is partly why I am here. There is a lot that all of us here want to see corrected. But I recall Winston Churchill, who said that democracy is the worst form of government, except for all the others. That is probably where most of us are.

"Sure, there is a lot that is wrong with our society. But also there is a lot of good here. Take, for example, the idea of rights. How many times did St. Paul claim his rights as a Roman citizen? Though he was critical of it, he appreciated what the Roman Empire did for him. That attitude permeates his writings, including Romans 13.

"I basically adhere to Richard John Neuhaus's vision of things.

Better than anyone else in our day, Neuhaus articulates what the relationship between the Church and the society should be. As I read him, there should be tension between the two. The realms of the Church and the society are distinct and separate, but they also must interact. We are both Christians and citizens. People in the church that I serve are policemen, politicians, and in the business world. The Church is not separate from the rest of culture. We are the culture."

Hauerwas responded: "I think the United States of America is a good place to live. Paul Van Buren, talking about theologians in the university, said, 'We do not need to bite the hand that feeds us, but we do not need to lick it either.' On the whole, Christians have licked the hand of the United States, and think of this as a Christian civilization. But this is not a Christian civilization. I think that America is preeminently a project of Enlightenment rationalism. It did not start out that way, but that is what it has become. And we are now paying the price for it, big time. At the heart of American civilization today is economics. In the name of freedom, there is a tendency to turn all relationships into contractual relationships. Unfortunately, this is succeeding. Economics is at the heart of the matter, and American economics is not now controlled politically."

Engaging Lindquist at various points, Hauerwas asserted that Roman rights differed from American rights. The Roman vision of social rights—in which duties were primarily important and determined correlative rights, which were secondarily important—has much to be said for it. America's understanding of rights, on the other hand, simply and mistakenly places rights over and above duties. Lindquist's two-realms description, according to Hauerwas, is just "corrupt Lutheranism."

Then said Hauerwas, "Don't quote Romans 13 to me after Nazi Germany. Romans 13, isolated from Revelation 13, is an invitation to the demonic. People forget that Hitler was the most democratically elected leader of this century. The fact that that was democracy does not impress me one bit. The issue is what kind of people they were.

"Can a Christian be a policeman? In a local congregation, you are going to have to worry about that. I would assume that policemen in the church bear the burden of proof. Policemen in the church might say, 'Because I do not want to use violence, I may have to risk my life more often. So, is the church ready to aid my family in the event of my death?' You see, I am not, in principle, opposed to Christians being policemen. It might actually work out."

With that, the session built around the Hauerwas paper, which had pushed for a reexamination of first principles on a wide range of issues, drew to a conclusion. Conference attention then shifted to more practical concerns.

BROWN ON MINISTRY

The fourth paper of the day, which was entitled "The Ministry of a Crisis Pregnancy Center," was written by Ruth Brown. Drawing from her experience in directing a crisis pregnancy center, Brown, who now directs the Taskforce of United Methodists on Abortion and Sexuality, was ready to suggest what the local church might do to provide ministry to those tempted by, and taken in by, abortion.

Brown began: "The silent cry of women in particularly difficult pregnancies today is, 'Does anyone hear, and does anyone care?' Up to now, The United Methodist Church has not responded to that cry. We will never stop abortion by simply arguing the merits of life over against abortion. We, as the Church, have to be willing to be out there providing support to girls, women, and families who are grappling for answers to the crisis pregnancies in their lives." As a model for church action, Brown described the work of Sav-A-Life Wiregrass of Dothan, Alabama. She pointed out "the remarkable difference that a little unconditional love can make in the life of a girl or a woman when she does not know where to turn."

Brown then stressed six themes that emerge from her paper. First, "the need for ministry is very real," even though the abortion problem is often hidden from the public eye. For abortion is usually sought and secured in secret. Second, "crisis pregnancy involves all levels of society. The citizens in our community wanted to think that only the unchurched, the poor, the welfare recipients, and the uneducated were ending up in crisis pregnancies. We were told that, through our ministry, we were just encouraging these women and girls to get pregnant. But that is not true. We saw people in our center from every level of society and from all walks of life—including young people who were church leaders. We tried to instill a sense of responsibility in the young people to take charge of their lives and turn them around." Third, "many women seek abortion, not because they want it, but because they come to see it as their only choice, not a choice." When offered hope in the form of friendship and alternatives to abortion, most women in crisis pregnancies quickly opt for the life of their children.

Brown's fourth theme was that adoption is a positive alternative to abortion. Even within some of the churches, a "guilt trip" was laid on many of the young women who had decided to put their babies up for adoption; these women were accused of being "unloving and uncaring." On the contrary, "The general public needs to understand that it requires more mature love for a girl to relinquish her baby in adoption than to keep and attempt to raise her child. This girl needs support, not condemnation." Fifth, "the Church has a role in teaching sexual morality. In Sunday school, children are taught to be kind, not to steal, not to lie, and so on. But also we need to teach them not to be involved in sex outside of marriage. God set the limits, not to restrict their pleasure, but to protect them, and to heighten the joy and commitment of oneness in marriage." Sixth, Brown said that, equipped by Christ, the Church can be at the forefront of life-saving ministries and moral teaching. If the Church can get over its habit of speaking about rights, it might be able to demonstrate mercy in a way that would make a difference for the good. "The Church needs to be a shelter to the lost, to the lonely, and to those looking for answers. The 'Sheltering Church' can provide that support, if we serve Christ by serving 'the least of these'—the unborn baby, the mother, the parents of the mother, the father, and the parents of the father."

Brown concluded her opening remarks: "In our work at the center, we found that the child is not the only victim of abortion. The women themselves become victims. Also society has been a victim of abortion. I grieve with my friends who will never know their grandchildren. And I have cried with grown men, who have been so guilty and had blood on their hands, as they described their participation in abortions during their college years; they paid for abortions rather than help women carry their children to term. Nineteen years of abortion on demand have left millions of silently grieving people in its wake. I pray that we, as the Church, will extend to them the unconditional love of Jesus Christ, his redemptive power, and the joy that is found only in a right relationship with him."

TELLING THE TRUTH

Les Longden, the first to comment on Brown's paper, referred to the so-called "gag rule" or Title 10, which presently prohibits birth-control clinics that are supported with federal dollars from mentioning abortion as an alternative. According to the pro-choice community, the gag rule prevents such clinics from passing along the whole truth to pregnant women.

But the truth, said Brown, is definitely not told by abortion clinics. According to Brown, young women who had gone to abortion clinics repeatedly reported that the abortion-clinic counseling they had received depicted abortion as painless and easy, "done under anesthetic, and over in a few minutes. That was the extent of the counseling. They were not told what was going to happen, what the ramifications would be. The clinics did not tell the women that their babies already had a heartbeat, or that their arms and legs were already formed. One or two of the women who visited our center called the clinic where they had had their abortions. They asked the clinic, 'Why didn't you tell me these things?' They were impatiently told, 'You came here wanting an abortion. We did what you asked us to do. If you are having problems, they are your problems, not ours.'"

The Reverend Constance Roland Alt followed by noting that, "in our society, abortion is the only surgery where the patient is not given full information. It is, in fact, an invasive procedure with instruments that are designed to eliminate the patient's baby. Abortion clinics, by the way, are not regulated by the medical profession in most states."

"Absolutely," Dr. Douglas agreed. "Abortion is the only medical procedure that is not regulated. And abortion clinics do not have to list, for their clients, the potential complications that accompany abortion." In addition, in many states, parental consent is not legally required for minors to obtain abortions. Therefore, "a girl has to get parental consent to have her ears pierced, but not to get an abortion," said Douglas. "Again, abortion clinics are not regulated in any fashion whatsoever."

Also, said Hauerwas and Douglas, the financial side of abortion should not be overlooked. After all, money is the main reason that abortion clinics are in business, Douglas argued.

Dr. Lisa Fair, a resident at Pitt Memorial County Hospital in Greenville, North Carolina, then spoke up about abortion and medical education. She said: "I struggled with the abortion issue when I began to think about obstetrics and gynecology as a profession. I still struggle with the hard cases. But I came to the perhaps naive conclusion that I could not say Yes to one woman who wanted an abortion and No to another. Therefore, I will not do abortions at all. That is still where I am.

"When I interviewed for residency in obstetrics and gynecology, I found that the vast majority of institutions do not require their residents to do abortions. Even at the University of North Carolina, Chapel Hill, which runs a large abortion clinic, the residents are not required to participate, if they desire not to. That is very encouraging to me.

"I am not forced to participate in abortions in Greenville. But I get challenged by my fellow residents every time I choose not to participate in an abortion. For example, I get asked, 'If you are not going to do anything about a baby with Down syndrome, then why are you going to do an amniocentesis?' My defense for that is that parents of a baby with Down syndrome, early in the pregnancy, might begin attending a support group.

"It is hard to be a resident. It is hard to be the only Christian in your residency group and not have anyone to help hold you up. You do feel lonely. You do feel scared, sometimes. But that is another place where your faith comes in. You have to stand on that rock, on that faith. God did not promise that the decisions that we make would be easy, but he did promise to be there when we made the hard ones. Therefore, I will stand my ground. When interviewing for a private-practice position, I plan to be upfront about this. I trust that God will open the doors to a practice that will accept my position on abortion."

"I want the kind of church," said Pastor Willimon, "where it would be a lot less lonely to take a stand like Lisa has. If John Wesley had any genius, it was, in a sense, a political genius. He had this vision that you could create new structures through which ordinary people could become saints and do some extraordinary things. But along the way, Christian theology and the Church got corrupted by Augustinians and Lutherans, who focus on the individual. Wesley had no such delusions. He knew you had better put people, even brave but lonely people, in a group. You see, Ruth Brown's vision is also a very Wesleyan, very Methodist, vision. You get these lonely young women, made more lonely by this tough dilemma that they are in, and you put them in a group.

"I am anxious for The Durham Declaration to move the church to examine ecclesial, political, social, and structural concerns that would enable people to be more courageous. Recently I met a guy at Duke who told me he was a Mormon. So I made some kind of ecumenical remark, like, 'But you seem so intelligent to be a Mormon; how did you get mixed up with the Mormons?' He said, 'I want to be a good husband. I want to be a good father. I am just an ordinary man. And I quickly found out that I do not have what I need to be a good husband or a good father. I am just not good at it. So we are in the church now, and the church is making me an incredibly good husband and father. I am down at the church four nights a week, and they train me in these things.'

"So I gave a nice, accommodationist response, 'Oh yea, you Mormons are like that. Closed off in your own little world.' And he said to me, 'All I have to say is that we are the only family on our street whose children have not been in trouble with the law or with drugs.' Well, I got to thinking about stopping somebody in eighteenth-century England and asking, 'How did you get mixed up with this sect, with these Methodists?' They might have replied, 'Well, I am just an ordinary person with a bad drinking problem, and now the Methodists have rearranged my social life and put me in a small group.' That is a very Wesleyan vision. Failing that, about all we United Methodists have left to do about abortion is offer some advice to Congress."

In Brown's paper, which concerns works of mercy, the first pastoral challenge is to tell the truth about abortion. "So often we see works of mercy as solely supportive and therapeutic," said the moderator. "But Ruth Brown's first merciful work is telling to tell the truth about what is involved in abortion."

"And the truth is on our side," said Jenks. Explaining to a

young woman in his congregation the mere facts of abortion, this pastor had found that the woman was immediately persuaded away from a hard pro-choice position.

HOPE AND REPENTANCE, AGAINST EVIL

Alt liked Brown's emphasis on hope. "You know," she said, "we Christians have cornered the market on hope. And yet, as a church, we say there are many situations that are hopeless. In our *Book of Discipline*, in the paragraph on abortion, we talk about 'tragic conflicts of life with life that may justify abortion.' *Tragedy* is a hard term to use when we are talking about life-giving and life-saving. If we Christians know anything about grace, how can we possibly speak about a hopeless situation? If God cannot extricate us from the worst of situations, he cannot extricate us from anything. Hope is the medicine for so many of our ills."

"In all of this," replied the Reverend Thomas Collins, "those of us around this table are trying to say that there are people within the church who will fall, who will stumble, who will fail, even leaders of the church. But we are calling the church to recognize Christ above the church and in the church, and above the Christian and in the Christian. And we need to continue to ask, What can the church do to faithfully be the Church?" Part of that, suggested Collins, is for the local congregation to offer works of mercy to the threatened unborn and to their mothers and fathers.

Then came Dr. John E. Horton, Jr. "As I reflect on what I have been experiencing during these six or more hours," he said, "one of the main things that I am feeling is dis-ease and frustration. Part of it is that, before now, I have not thought radically enough about what it means to be the Church and to be baptized. I have not enjoyed hearing much of what I have heard today, because this has called me to repentance. It is easy to preach that abortion is sinful and that murdering children is wrong. But by and large, I have been content to stop there and have been unwilling to pay the price of inviting a young, single mother, who has an unwanted pregnancy, into my home to take care of her. I have not been willing to say, 'This is our child, who will be assisted with our money.'

"I have not been willing to pay the price of our convictions.

133

Our denomination, as an institution with its systems, has not been willing to pay the price of calling our people to accountability with regard to abortion, privatization, and individualization. Now all of a sudden, when we are expecting and demanding things of our people that had not been mentioned when they joined the church, too many of our people, since we have done such a poor job of teaching, will probably feel like we are changing the rules in the middle of the ball game. They might well say to us, 'Well, nobody talked to me about this when I joined the church.' So, exactly how do we affect a change of heart?

"Every battle, my wife has taught me, must be fought in the spirit and in the flesh. Well, I am not a pietist; I wish I were more pietistic. I am an activist. But I am growing in the realization that it has always been too easy for me to face problems like abortion on the social, ecclesiastical, and political levels. Today, for example, I came here hoping that we would spend part of our time strategizing about how we would achieve changes in The United Methodist Church at the 1992 General Conference. But today we have spent a lot of our time considering the things of the spirit. Mike Gorman and Stan Hauerwas mentioned the 'directorate of death.' We might go further and talk about the forces of evil and satan. We have to fight these forces on every front, without assuming that some change of wording in the Social Principles of The United Methodist Church would be the victory. That would be a small thing when compared with our church becoming, in reality, the People of God, the Family of God."

Lindquist commented that he enjoyed Brown's paper, in part because it was not heavy with theology. Then he quoted a passage: "Satan's answers are so easy at the beginning and so hard at the end."

"But that's theology," chimed in Boothby to a round of conference laughter.

Lindquist agreed, and proceeded to underline the "evil of abortion." He noted that there is something nearly demonic about abortion.

Asked about how it was that she entered the Sav-A-Life ministry, Ruth Brown answered, "Through a series of major attacks, culminating in the death of my husband in 1974, I found that satan is a liar, that God is real, and that my faith was strong. At the time my husband died, I had four sons, and the youngest was six. At that time, I knew that if God was not real, I was not going to make it. I told him then, 'I depend on you. I will not refuse to go through a door you open. I will look to you and not to myself.'" Brown then went on to work at a financial institution, and thereby learned the ropes of the business world, which she would later apply to a crisis pregnancy center and to the Taskforce.

SLAVERY AS CHOICE

Willimon then brought up the slavery connection. "The way The Durham Declaration referred to slavery," he said, "was wonderful." Slavery is a powerful analogy. Methodists in England were never allowed to hold slaves. But when we arrived in this new democracy, we found that everybody who was anybody did a little slavery on the side—Thomas Jefferson, George Washington, and so on. We quickly found out that if you are going to have power, then you had better be willing to do a little slavery. Therefore, we voted to make slavery a personal decision. When Methodists did that, the jig was up and we would swallow practically anything.

"We United Methodists are part of a vision that Wesley had. When Wesley read, 'Be ye perfect, as your Father in heaven is perfect' in the Sermon on the Mount, he did not say, like we do, 'Jesus, what did you mean by perfect? We cannot take that literally. And on and on.' Instead, Wesley stepped back and asked, 'What kind of church would you have to have to take this commandment seriously? It is not the church that I know. It is some other church.' So, we might ask what kind of church would it take to include a Ruth Brown, so that she would not be out there alone."

Wesleyan Methodists, Willimon clarified, abided by the notion that John Wesley did not want his people to own slaves. Therefore, they withdrew from the Methodist Episcopal Church. "Unfortunately, I was always told that Wesleyan Methodists were just those folks who did not allow drinking. Nobody ever told me why that break really occurred." And the ramifications of that break are still with our church today, said Willimon: "The United

Methodist Church of the present was born in the nineteenth century's debate over slavery. Once our church made slavery a private issue, we could make sex a personal-private issue. That, fundamentally, is the wrong turn we took. The Durham Declaration raised this big specter and asked, Haven't we had this discussion before?"

Simpson mentioned that "the Methodist Episcopal Church never took the prohibition against slaveholding out of its *Book of Discipline*. We suspected slavery was wrong. We knew it was wrong. Because of the book, we knew it was wrong. But we continued to do it, because it was convenient, expedient, and economically advantageous. So we, in the South, lived a life of duplicity. This was addressed, but not settled, by the Civil War. In 1939, when the Methodist Episcopal Church, South and the Methodist Episcopal Church united, it was addressed again but not fully resolved. We, as a church, did a better job of it in the 1968 union. It took us that long to grapple with the problems raised by slavery."

Willimon shifted the conversation back to the present: "A couple of weeks ago a United Methodist bishop was bragging to me that the beautiful thing was that we United Methodists had decided not to talk about abortion. He said that that is a good thing. I asked him why. And he said, 'It could blow us apart.' I suppose that is a good reason why we do not talk about a lot of stuff. We are afraid that if we, who now have so little holding us together, put that on the table, it could blow up in our faces."

The moderator followed by telling about his work on a conference committee that was looking into retirement-home ministries. "I am of the opinion," he said, "that in laying out the vision for United Methodist retirement homes that we, as a church, come clean on the problem of euthanasia. That is, we as a church should state that in our retirement homes, we would not have doctors, nurses, or workers intentionally taking life. After raising this point at a committee meeting, a couple committee members looked up and said, 'We cannot do that. If that kind of a statement was taken to the floor of annual conference, that is all that would get discussed.' We Methodists are afraid of the issues where we are called to take a principled, clearly delineated position."

Looking at Hauerwas, the pacifist, Robb said that "some around this table are uncomfortable with militaristic terms. But we are going to win the battle over abortion in The United Methodist Church and, for those of us concerned with this, in the United States at large. In fifty years, elective abortion will be illegal in every state, county, and municipality in the United States. Far before that, God willing, it will be properly condemned in our church. We will have set up save-a-baby ministries and changed our ethos in other ways. The reason I believe this is the abolitionist example.

"Abolitionists got going a long time before slavery was abolished. It was not until the early 1800s that abolitionists spoke out in Boston, the only place where they would not get lynched. Even in New York and other centers of elite eastern culture, abolitionism was seen as the worst possible alternative, because it was divisive, would break up the country, and would cause a war. To the extent that the country gave into that, we made the Civil War inevitable later on, because the conflict just got bigger and bigger, until it exploded. But some things are just too evil to stand. And abortion is one of them; it will not stand. But in the meantime, it is going to take people who are willing to be lonely and lynched, so to speak, to take the stand."

Douglas added that it took twenty years of struggle—and mainly prayer and prayer vigils, for hours a day—for William Wilberforce, also using democratic means, to overturn slavery in England. Douglas, of course, was expressing the hope that that history would inform the present moment.

THE EPISCOPAL SILENCE

William Simpson spoke about abortion as a cause of high-risk sexual behavior, that in turn spreads sexually transmitted diseases such as AIDS. He also emphasized the importance of the Church addressing, in a forceful way, Christian sexual morals, which is one of the concerns of The Durham Declaration.

The Reverend Presnell then began a new line of inquiry: "Is it too much to expect the hierarchy of our church to take a bold stand on abortion and sexuality? Why is it that our bishops will not speak to these issues? How can we encourage the bishops and the church to make pastoral statements about these matters? I feel like many of our people are floundering. And a lot of our clergy are not bold simply because we do not have the structure to uphold us as we proclaim the gospel."

Here Heidinger pointed out a problem: "We have got a credibility problem when we think about ministry, as Ruth Brown has depicted it, that goes against the church's stated positions. Recently I read a full-page ad in a newspaper for the Religious Coalition for Abortion Rights (RCAR). It listed the two United Methodist agencies that are members of RCAR [the General Board of Church and Society, and the Women's Division of the General Board of Global Ministries] and are probably still on its letterhead. It is a problem for us to affirm abortion-prevention ministry, on the one hand, and not come to grips with our church's institutions that are supporting permissive life-styles, on the other. None of us likes confrontation. But we have a problem within our own fellowship that we are going to have to address somehow." This is nothing new, as Heidinger pointed to the arguments between Peter and Paul over the meaning of the gospel. "It is easier to think about compassionate ministry than to confront the unpleasantness of dealing with what we have in our church. At this point, lack of courage can become a moral and spiritual problem."

Then the moderator questioned Bishop Borgen, "Why is there a timidity among most United Methodism's bishops, active and retired, to engage the basic problems of sexual permissiveness and abortion? Why is there hesitation? Indeed, why is there silence?"

Borgen replied, "There may be many reasons for this. First of all, there has been a tendency in the church to isolate the bishops and take away from them the responsibility, and even the authority, to do what they once did. The General Conference of 1972 was very anti-episcopal, and this has continued over the years. Today we bishops do not have many tools to work with. Second, since I am one of those who feel that we should speak up, I think I can say also that there is a desire, among the bishops, to want to serve the whole church, all factions of the church, and to avoid being identified with one element of the church. Third, the Council of Bishops is nothing but a microcosm of the church. We are not all of one mind. We do not all come from the same starting point, and we do not all draw the same conclusions. The tensions in the church at large are reflected also in the Council of Bishops." Fourth, Borgen noted "political correctness," including the fear of being accused of sexism, as an inhibiting factor. Fifth and finally he said, "I personally feel that it is time for the whole church to come to the bishops and ask them to be accommodating no longer. We need to stand up and let the chips fall where they will."

"I would like to commend you, Bishop Borgen, for the courage that you have displayed in identifying yourself with The Durham Declaration project," said the moderator.

"That is not courage at all," Borgen shot back. "You have to remember that when these matters about abortion were brought up at the 1970 General Conference, the Europeans passed a resolution for inclusion in the *Daily Christian Advocate*, or in the minutes, that said we would not abide by decision of the General Conference." They did this, Borgen continued, on the basis of their experience of abortion in European societies. The General Conference action on abortion, which could be understood as pro-choice in orientation, contradicted "the way we European Methodists had been living and teaching for a long time."

"Well, Bishop Borgen, since you would not accept my compliment, I am going to argue with you," the moderator said to some laughter. "I would urge you, bishop, to reconsider your statement about how the Council of Bishops does not have many tools that could get your message out to the church. If we take seriously ordination to Word and Sacrament ministry, that ministry involves great, God-given authority and power. If we also take seriously consecration to the episcopal office, that involves great, God-given authority and power. Couple that with the publishing possibilities of the bishops, and there is tremendous power at the disposal of our bishops. At times, the Council of Bishops has taken hold of that power—for example, in the In Defense of Creation project, the anti-nuclear-war project. In that project, the council was responding, however adequately or inadequately, to a perceived crisis. The same tools can be employed in other areas with equal effectiveness."

"The only means we bishops have is the way of prescription," replied the bishop. "But we can individually stand up and be counted. Furthermore, I cannot live with myself if I cannot have peace with God. That is why I have to sometimes go against the currents. If I cannot have peace with God, my life is shot."

Roman Catholic Bishop F. Joseph Gossman then entered the conversation, "During this conference I have been sitting here quietly, because I came here to listen. I have learned quite a bit. I have learned that there are different ways of looking at the abortion question. I doubt that most of what I have listened to, learned, and read about abortion in my church has approached abortion in exactly the same way as today's papers have. That is helpful, because we all get so blinded by our own church's viewpoint and forget that there are other ways to skin a cat.

"One of the most simple but penetrating remarks that I heard recently about abortion is that abortion is about death. Our society would like us to think that it is about a lot of other things and issues. But it is always about death. I am not sure we say that often enough. We get caught up in the linguistics of society. But we have to decide where the argument is and be willing to keep it there. Another problem is that today people do not talk to each other; they talk at each other. They never really connect, especially on this issue. I wish I could tell you how to change that."

Reverend Oliver concluded the fourth part of the conference: "My own ministry relates to retarded persons. I am impressed with the sheer number of so-called unlovely people out in the communities where we live. Because they are unlovely, because they do not think like we do, they do not get brought into our churches. Let me plead with you: we are called by Christ to love those who are unlovely, those who do not think like we do, and those who might want to hurt us." Sad to say, most clergy, Oliver said, cannot even identify these people in their midst. But it is time for us to call these people—those called retarded and those called unwanted—to Christ and his Church.

With that, the conference then turned to presentations by four panelists.

THE PANEL OF FOUR

LISTENING TO WOMEN

The first panelist was Kathy Rudy. She said: "On the cover of the book *Abortion in a Roman Catholic Perspective*, there is a picture, taken from the Sistine Chapel, of fingers touching between Adam and God. In my work on abortion during the past four years, I feel like that is exactly what is going on in the discussion of abortion—women are not at all represented. The conversation happens between mankind and God, or between men and men. But women have a different voice and need a special space to be heard.

"The difference has a lot to do with our inability to talk about sexuality. *Roe v. Wade* was handed down when I was seventeen. I remember being incredibly embarrassed soon thereafter when people explained to me precisely what abortion was. It was something that I did not want to talk about. That, I am afraid, persists in our churches. But today there is no embarrassment in our high schools, in our bedrooms, and in our families. Today sexuality is not something we, in the Church, can avoid talking about.

"Interviewing people who are entering abortion clincs, I have found that, when there were protesters outside, they said, 'The offer of help I heard from the protesters was okay, but I wish I had heard it earlier. The time to get support from Christians is not the minute I am going into an abortion clinic. It only made me feel bad.'

"About two years ago I was walking another woman into an abortion clinic located between Durham and Chapel Hill. A person from my department at Duke said to her, 'Come live with us.' But it was too late. The series of decisions had already been made. The offer has to come sooner.

"In response to what has been presented here today, I want to point out that tough love cannot happen only on the site of my body. It has got to involve all of us. We need to think not only about opposing abortions individually but also about sustaining women and their children with our money. We need to pay their rent and buy their groceries. But that is not enough. If I am pregnant, if I am faced with the possibility of losing a year of school and being pushed out of my family, paying my rent is not enough. Why don't we talk about each of us giving $1,000 right here and now to a fund that would save six children? That is the kind of toughness that we need to support. We are talking big money. As a feminist, I support what has been said here. But I would caution against pushing women too quickly into the site of tough love."

MAKING CONNECTIONS

Recalling the purpose of the conference—changing the heart and mind, and the teaching and practice, of the church on the abortion problem, Martha Clark Boothby discussed adoption, ownership of the body, and poverty and infant mortality. "Stanley Hauerwas and Will Willimon raised adoption as a part of our baptismal covenant and our life together as Christians. As Christians, if we are to hold up adoption as the first form of parenting, as Stanley says, we have to look more closely at how our culture is teaching people to understand adoption. On this I want to use two illustrations that I have seen in the past year. The first was a television news story. The undercurrent of the line of questioning in the interviews of the biological parents was, How can you possibly live with the decision to give up your children for adoption? Or, How can you live with this guilt? Or, Isn't there something a little perverse, wrong, un-American, and anti-family about your decision? Obviously, the interviewed families had struggled with this. But they realized, in a very mature way, that there were good people out there who wanted to take their children. And second, I know one of the women at the student health facility at Duke. She sees a lot of the women who come in for crisis pregnancy counseling. There is an average of one positive pregnancy test a day at the United Methodist institution called Duke University. And yet, as she says, there are no pregnant undergraduates. You just do not see them walking around. Nearly all opt for abortion. In my friend's experience, there has been only one who has dropped out of school to have her child. In laying out all the options to these women, my friend said that she found 'adoption was the most abhorrent alternative.' Why is that? Well, we need to start thinking about that. On the issue of adoption, our culture is thinking something very different. If we think we are going to offer adoption as a real alternative to the problem of abortion, we are going to have to get into yet another battle."

On the idea that Christians do not own their bodies, which The Durham Declaration advances, Boothby said, "That is not a new message to women. Women have never owned their bodies. We have been property throughout history. The Christian women's struggle today is not necessarily to own our bodies, but to own the stewardship of our bodies. Men have not been good examples to us on stewardship of our bodies. It is up to us, as Christian women, to teach people—and that includes our brother Christians—what it means to be stewards of our bodies. The new message coming out of the churches is that our bodies are good and that they are a gift. It is obvious that we in the Church have often carried a very skewed, wounded story about sexuality and the body that has been passed down to us. It is time to proclaim the goodness of our bodies in creation, and to live that fully. The ramifications of that, with regard to abortion, are certainly open to discussion."

Boothby concluded on poverty and infant mortality. "Last week-end I went to an Episcopal Church conference on infant mortality in North Carolina. Earlier today several have said that the Church needs to properly condemn abortion. Well, I am convinced that poverty needs to be properly condemned before we can properly condemn abortion. Looking at infant mortality in North Carolina, you find that 15,000 die before the age of one every year; forty-one children have died today, mostly because of health-related problems. Those are realities that the Church and the medical establishment can work on together. I do not think that forty-one children have to die every day in North Carolina. In addition, in the state of North Carolina, 45,000 children a year are born with preventable disabilities. How can we preach pro-life and not insist that our churches deal with the issues of poverty?"

A FEMINIST FOR LIFE

The Reverend Constance Roland Alt was the third panelist to speak. "Implied but not stated explicitly in the four conference papers is an extremely bothersome situation. They imply that mainline Protestantism, namely The United Methodist Church, is waging war against women. We, as United Methodists, have served and are serving the evils we deplore, to use Harry Emerson Fosdick's wording from the hymn 'God of Grace and God of Glory.' We participate in these atrocities daily. We have capitulated to the forces that deny freedom and destroy life. We are captors and oppressors. Now I do not find this strong language in any of the papers. But how else do you describe this reality that we are in, unless you use the language of warfare?

"Our church is not warring against principalities and powers here. We are warring against women. So let's be honest. When such destruction and disruption of lives and families take place by deliberate, calculated methods and tools, it is nothing but war. And a terribly dirty one at that. With its attendant terrorism, propaganda, disinformation, captivity, and slaughter of the innocent—that's war. The state of affairs is so grave and massive that we, the people of the resurrection, have even contributed to what might be called a death system. But we fail to call death 'death.' There is, among us, death but no grief; indeed, there is a denial of the expression of grief. There was a death system, like today's, in the Middle Ages during the bubonic plague. Then there was so massive a destruction going on that there was no time to grieve. In such circumstances, a societal mythology has to be developed so that people can deal with it. That is an awful indictment against us Easter people.

"Back to the warfare and the evils. What are they, besides weak resignation?

"Sexism is one evil. Despite the rallying cry of more well-known, so-called feminist spokespersons, the fact stands that women will remain second-class citizens as long as they are seen as requiring surgery in order to avoid their biological gifts, in order to avoid their expression of who they are deep inside of themselves. We are women. Our abortion mentality says, 'No. That is inconvenient. Be unpregnant like we men. We do not get pregnant. You do. Handle it. Take care of it. Get yourself vacuumed out.' Here there is a denial and fear of our fundamental identity as human beings.

"Terrorism. Remember the movie Sophie's Choice, where a woman is forced to make a decision between loved ones? There is nothing but terrorism going on when a husband or a boyfriend or a father says to a woman, 'I will withdraw my love and support for you if you do not destroy this child.' That is terrorism. It is certainly terrorism to go after, with sharp instruments or a very high-powered vacuum cleaner, an innocent human being.

"Ageism is another evil. That child is still a child from the moment of conception, even if the child is too small to fight against us.

"Elitism. This church participates not in inclusiveness but in elitism when it comes to the issue of abortion. We participate in supporting male dominance. We participate in telling the poor, 'We will not help you get some relief. We would rather that you kill your babies.' So the Religious Coalition for Abortion Rights tried and tried to get government funding restored so that the poor can abort their babies, too. It is elitism against the handicapped, against those we cannot see, against the unwanted. This elitism involves a utilitarian ethic that is patently un-Christian. It assumes that you are valuable only so long as you can produce goods and services. So it is okay to kill the poor and the handicapped, because they are not fit. This is murder of the innocents as a solution, which is typically and historically a male solution to problems.

"Racism. Not all of the poor in this country are people of color. But you had better believe that that is part of the pro-abortion agenda. And that is part of the original agenda of Planned Parenthood, in which Margaret Sanger declared that we need to get rid of these undesirables, which were assumed to be black people.

"Oppression. This includes economic oppression. It is ironic indeed that women have bought into this oppression mentality. The only way to explain it is that they are sympathizing with their kidnappers. Hostages that are taken hostage will often eventually develop a syndrome in which they sympathize with their captors. That is one reason that women might betray who they are.

"Violence. Abortion is violence against or destruction of the past, community, hope, and the future. Serving the God whom we adore means serving, welcoming, making room, and establishing a home. And for the unborn child, the womb is home.

"Another evil of abortion is unredemptive victimization. A lesser evil is patronization.

"There are many evils. And we are battling flesh and blood. We are battling against women. We are in warfare against them. Why is that? I do not know, other than that we have always been aggressive as people. We have always been sinful. We have glorified the survival of the fittest. We are a utilitarian society, and we are becoming more utilitarian, as we experiment with embryos and edge closer to euthanasia. Then again, maybe we wage war against women because they are very powerful. But we have always done that. For women have an awesome power, which is a gift from God: the ability to bear children. That is power indeed. Either this has been held in awe and reverence, or it has been denigrated and clamped down upon. Women are perceived to be a threat. We always have been and probably always will be."

Taking a line from Danny Glover in the movie *Grand Canyon*, Roland concluded, "'Hey man, it ain't supposed to be like this.' So that is what I say. We should not be waging war against women and their children. And darned if we have not participated in this war as a church."

THE CHURCH'S ADVANTAGE

Reverend Pat Tony, the fourth panelist, admitted that, in the light of the day's discussion, she had been challenged to begin rethinking the meaning of true compassion. She continued: "According to Will Willimon, God sends us the people we need to become the Church. That means that we, as Church, must be open to the helpless and the unlovely among us. Also, we already have what we need to be a faith-full Church. That is the important thing. For when Jesus returns, the overriding question is, Will he find faith upon the earth (Luke 18)? We are the people who have the story of hope, healing, reconciliation, and all the things that people really need.

"We also have the calling to be a community of character, Stanley Hauerwas reminds us. One of the chief virtues of that kind of community is hospitality, as we have been reminded today. Hand in hand with hospitality is education. The Church must teach about sexuality from the Church's moral-theological foundation. Here I would emphasize the character of God. When we speak about God's commandments, we need to recognize that along with God's negative command comes his positive and protective provisions for people. 'Thou shalt not' commit sexual sin comes from provisions of the covenant of marriage and the gift of celibacy.

"In order for people to see and trust the God of the covenant, we must put feet to our prayers. After all, people do not care how much we know until they know how much we care. We trust God for the grace to live as a covenant community.

"The problem of abortion is, of course, much larger than The United Methodist Church. Therefore, we are thankful that today God appears to be moving to join the Body of Christ together across denominational lines. This looks like a worldwide work of the Holy Spirit. I attended a conference last November that involved about ten thousand people from more than eighty countries. There were many races and cultures represented. But we all had one thing in common—the cross of Jesus Christ. One of the conference songs went like this: 'Meet me at the cross, where it all began . . . Meet me where His blood makes us family, one race, holy through His grace.' The song also talks about our bloodshed and streets strewn with violence that we have committed against one another. But if we can come together at the cross, forgiveness is there. Hope is there. Through the blood of Jesus Christ, healing and reconciliation are there.

"Someone has said that we can accomplish a lot by God's grace if we do not care who gets the credit. Abortion is a problem of such magnitude and evil that it compels us to join hands and prayerfully do battle in the spirit and in the flesh."

Dr. Horton fittingly concluded the conference with prayer: "Our heavenly Father, we come to you with hearts that are stirred and moved and troubled. You have troubled us once again. We are grateful for that, because until we are troubled we cannot understand a new challenge, we cannot adopt a new language to deal with a problem in a new and fresh way. Grant us hope, and grant us vision. Enable us to trust you to know that you bless faithfulness. Enable us to know that our major task is not to be successful in this warfare, but to be faithful, and that you will take care of the success or failure. Take that which we have sought to offer you and use it to bless your Church afresh. Amen."

And Amen.

—CONFERENCE PARTICIPANTS—

Ms. Patricia O'Brien Aiken
Annapolis, Maryland

The Reverend Constance Roland Alt
Christ United Methodist Church
Wilmington, Delaware

The Reverend David A. Banks
Saint Peter's United Methodist Church
Morehead City, North Carolina

The Reverend Randy C. Blanchard
Edenton Street United Methodist Church
Raleigh, North Carolina

Ms. Martha Clark Boothby
The Divinity School
Duke University
Durham, North Carolina

Bishop Ole E. Borgen
Asbury Theological Seminary
Wilmore, Kentucky, and Lillestrom, Norway

Ms. Ruth S. Brown
Taskforce of United Methodists on Abortion and Sexuality
Dothan, Alabama

Ms. Anna G. Collins
Raleigh, North Carolina

The Reverend Thomas A. Collins
Layden Memorial United Methodist Church
Raleigh, North Carolina

The Reverend Clyde A. Denny
Ocracoke United Methodist Church
Ocracoke, North Carolina

Mr. Thomas Donelson
Olathe, Kansas

Dr. Edgar S. Douglas, Jr.
Greenville Obstetrics and Gynecology, P.A.
Greenville, North Carolina

Dr. Lisa A. Fair
Pitt County Memorial Hospital
Greenville, North Carolina

Dr. Michael J. Gorman
The Ecumenical Institute of Theology
St. Mary's Seminary and University
Baltimore, Maryland

Bishop F. Joseph Gossman
Diocese of Raleigh
Raleigh, North Carolina

The Reverend Walter D. Graham III
Louisa United Methodist Church
Louisa, Virginia

Professor Stanley Hauerwas
The Divinity School
Duke University
Durham, North Carolina

Ms. Elizabeth B. Haugh
Kitty Hawk United Methodist Church
Kitty Hawk, North Carolina

The Reverend James V. Heidinger II
Good News
Wilmore, Kentucky

The Reverend John E. Horton, Jr.
First United Methodist Church
Albany, Georgia

The Reverend Eddie Jo V. Jarrett
Lakewood United Methodist Church
Durham, North Carolina

The Reverend Gregory K. Jenks
Saxapahaw United Methodist Church
Saxapahaw, North Carolina

The Reverend Carl W. Lindquist
Bethany United Methodist Church
Lexington, North Carolina

The Reverend Leicester R. Longden
Office of the Chaplain
Drew University
Madison, New Jersey

The Reverend Richard McClain
The Mission Society for United Methodists
Decatur, Georgia

The Reverend Thomas G. Melvin
Lakeview United Church of Canada
Calgary, Alberta
Canada

The Reverend William L. Oliver, Jr.
Wesley Glen Ministries with Retarded Persons
Albany, Georgia

The Reverend E. Powell Osteen, Jr.
Resurrection United Methodist Church
Durham, North Carolina

The Reverend J. Malloy Owen III
Goldsboro District of The United Methodist Church
Goldsboro, North Carolina

Ms. Patricia S. Owen
Goldsboro, North Carolina

The Reverend Dr. William M. Presnell
Kitty Hawk United Methodist Church
Kitty Hawk, North Carolina

Mr. James S. Robb
Bristol House, Ltd.
Lexington, Kentucky

Ms. Kathy Rudy
Graduate School
Duke University
Durham, North Carolina

The Reverend Dr. William C. Simpson, Jr.
Edenton Street United Methodist Church
Raleigh, North Carolina

The Reverend Paul T. Stallsworth
Creswell United Methodist Charge
Creswell, North Carolina

The Reverend Rufus H. Stark II
Methodist Home for Children
Raleigh, North Carolina

The Reverend Alan P. Swartz
New Hope United Methodist Church
Goldsboro, North Carolina

The Reverend Stephen L. Swecker [as reporter]
The United Methodist Reporter
Dallas, Texas

The Reverend Pat B. Tony
Bedford United Methodist Circuit
Bedford, Virginia

The Reverend Dr. William H. Willimon
Duke University Chapel
Durham, North Carolina

The Reverend Mathew Woodley
Barnum United Methodist Church
Barnum, Minnesota